Collins

KS3 Revision
Maths
Advanced

Maths

Advanced

KS3

Revision
Guide

**Samya Abdullah, Rebecca Evans
and Gillian Spragg**

Contents

N Number   **A** Algebra   **G** Geometry and Measures

Contents

S Statistics   **P** Probability   **R** Ratio, Proportion and Rates of change

Contents

N Number   **A** Algebra   **G** Geometry and Measures

Contents

S Statistics   **P** Probability   **R** Ratio, Proportion and Rates of change

Number 1

You must be able to:

- Carry out calculations with negative numbers
- Multiply and divide integers
- Carry out operations following BIDMAS.

Negative Numbers

- An **integer** is a whole number.
- Negative numbers are numbers less than zero.

Negative numbers | **Positive** numbers

−10 −9 −8 −7 −6 −5 −4 −3 −2 −1 0 1 2 3 4 5 6 7 8 9 10

- **Symbols** can be used to state the relationship between two numbers.

Symbol	Meaning
>	Greater than
<	Less than
≥	Greater than or equal to
≤	Less than or equal to
=	Equal to
≠	Not equal to

> **Example**
> −5 is greater than −10 can be written as −5 > −10

- When carrying out calculations with negative numbers the table below shows the rules.
- When adding and subtracting negative numbers the rules only apply if the signs are next to each other.

	+	−
+	+	−
−	−	+

Example
$-5 \times -3 = +15$
$-20 \div 4 = -5$
$-6 - (+5) = -6 - 5 = -11$
$-6 + 9 = 3$

Multiplication and Division

- To multiply large numbers using the grid method, partition both numbers into their hundreds, tens and units.

Key Point

There is an infinite number of positive and negative numbers.

Example

Calculate 354×273

354 is made up of 3 hundreds (300), 5 tens (50) and 4 units (4).

273 is made up of 2 hundreds (200), 7 tens (70) and 3 units (3).

×	300	50	4
200	60 000	10 000	800
70	21 000	3500	280
3	900	150	12

Complete the multiplication grid, for example **50 × 70 = 3500** and **4 × 3 = 12**

Then add together the numbers in the grid:

$60\,000 + 10\,000 + 800 + 21\,000 + 3500 + 280 + 900 + 150 + 12$

$= 96\,642$

So $354 \times 273 = \mathbf{96\,642}$

- Division can also be broken down into steps.

Example

$762 \div 3$

$3\overline{)7\,6\,2}$	$\begin{array}{c}2\\3\overline{)7\,{}^16\,2}\end{array}$	$\begin{array}{c}2\ 5\\3\overline{)7\,{}^16\,{}^12}\end{array}$	$\begin{array}{c}2\ 5\ 4\\3\overline{)7\,{}^16\,{}^12}\end{array}$
Set up your division.	Work out how many 3s go into 7. 3 goes into 7 twice with 1 left over. You carry the 1 over.	Work out how many 3s go into 16. 3 goes into 16 five times with 1 left over. You carry the 1 over.	Work out how many 3s go into 12. 3 goes into 12 four times with zero left over. So **762 ÷ 3 = 254**

BIDMAS

- BIDMAS gives the order in which operations should be carried out:

Brackets
Indices
Divide
Multiply
Add
Subtract

Example

$4 \times 5 + 6^2 \div 4$

$= 4 \times 5 + 36 \div 4$

$= 20 + 9$

$= 29$

Key Point

Indices are also called powers.

Quick Test

1. Work out -5×-7
2. Work out 435×521
3. Work out $652 \div 4$
4. Work out $4 \times 3^2 + 7 \times 4$

Key Words

integer
negative
positive

Number 2

You must be able to:

- Understand square numbers and square roots
- Write a number as a product of prime factors
- Find the lowest common multiple and highest common factor.

Squares and Square Roots

- **Square numbers** are calculated by multiplying a number by itself.

  Example

  $5^2 = 5 \times 5 = 25$

  ← This is a perfect square.

- A **square root** is the inverse or opposite of a square.

  Example

  $\sqrt{36} = 6$

- Not all square roots are integers and they can be approximated by a decimal.

  Example

  $\sqrt{6} = 2.45$ to 2 d.p.

Prime Factors

- **Factors** are numbers you can multiply together to make another number.
- Every number can be written as a **product** of prime factors.
- A **prime** number has exactly two factors, itself and 1.

Key Point

Product means multiply.

  Example

  45 can be expressed as a product of prime factors.

  This is called a **prime factor tree**.

$45 = 5 \times 9$

and

$9 = 3 \times 3$

← Always start by finding a prime number which is a factor, in this case 5.

So $45 = 3 \times 3 \times 5$

← Remember to write the final answer as a product.

Lowest Common Multiple and Highest Common Factor

- The **lowest common multiple** (LCM) is the lowest multiple two or more numbers have in common.
- The **highest common factor** (HCF) is the highest factor two or more numbers have in common.

Example

Find the lowest common multiple and highest common factor of 12 and 42.

Write both numbers as a product of prime factors.

$$12 = 2 \times 2 \times 3 \qquad 42 = 2 \times 3 \times 7$$

Complete the Venn diagram.

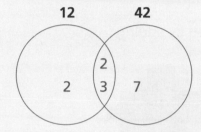

Common factors are placed in the overlap.

- The LCM is the product of all the numbers in both circles.

    $$\textbf{LCM} = 2 \times 2 \times 3 \times 7 = 84$$

- The HCF is the product of the numbers in the overlap.

    $$\textbf{HCF} = 2 \times 3 = 6$$

- LCM and HCF are used to solve many everyday problems.

Example

Thomas is training to swim the English Channel. He has to visit his doctor every 12 days and his nutritionist every 15 days. If, on October 1st, he has both appointments on the same day, on what date will he next have both appointments on the same day?

Find the LCM of 12 and 15. This is 60.

60 days after October 1st is November 30th.

Quick Test

1. Write down the value of 7^2.
2. Write down the value of $\sqrt{64}$.
3. Write 40 as a product of prime factors.
4. Find the lowest common multiple of 14 and 36.
5. Find the highest common factor of 24 and 32.

Key Words

square number
square root
factor
product
prime
lowest common multiple
highest common factor

Sequences 1

You must be able to:

- Recognise arithmetic and geometric sequences
- Generate sequences from a term to term rule
- Find missing terms in a sequence.

Algebra

Sequences

- A **sequence** is a set of shapes or numbers which follow a pattern or rule.
- The outputs from a **function machine** form a sequence.

> **Example**
>
> In the sequence below, the next pattern is formed by adding an extra layer of tiles around the previous pattern.
>
>
>
> Basic design   Layer 1   Layer 2   Layer 3
>   6 new tiles   10 new tiles   14 new tiles
>
> With each new layer the number of new tiles needed to increase by 4.
>
> This pattern can be used to predict how many tiles will be needed to make larger designs.

- An **arithmetic sequence** is a set of numbers with a common difference between consecutive terms.

> **Example**
>
> 4, 7, 10, 13, 16,…is an arithmetic sequence with a common difference of 3.
>
> 12, 8, 4, 0, –4,…is also an arithmetic sequence with a common difference of –4.

- A **geometric sequence** is a set of numbers where each term is found by multiplying the previous term by a constant.

> **Example**
>
> 3, 9, 27, 81,…is a geometric sequence where the previous term is multiplied by 3 to find the next term.
>
> 12, 6, 3, 1.5,…is also a geometric sequence where the previous term is multiplied by $\frac{1}{2}$ to find the next term.

 Key Point

There are many other types of sequences, for example square numbers, exponentials and reciprocals.

- When calculating terms of a geometric sequence, it is quicker to use powers.
- Arithmetic and geometric sequences are used to solve many everyday real-life problems.

Remember, $x^4 = x \times x \times x \times x$, $x^5 = x \times x \times x \times x \times x$

Example

A culture of bacteria **doubles** every 4 hours. If there are 1000 bacteria at the beginning, how many will there be in 12 hours?

$12 \div 4 = 3$, so it will double three times.

$1000 \times 2^3 = 8000$ bacteria

$2^3 = 2 \times 2 \times 2$

Finding Missing Terms

- The **term to term rule** links each term in the sequence to the previous term.

Example

$5, 6\frac{1}{3}, 7\frac{2}{3}, 9, 10\frac{1}{3}, \ldots$

In this set of numbers the next term is found by adding $1\frac{1}{3}$ to the previous term. Therefore the term to term rule is $+1\frac{1}{3}$

This rule can be used to find the next numbers in the sequence:

$10\frac{1}{3} + 1\frac{1}{3} = 11\frac{2}{3}$ $11\frac{2}{3} + 1\frac{1}{3} = 13$ $13 + 1\frac{1}{3} = 14\frac{1}{3}$

Therefore the next three terms in the sequence are

$11\frac{2}{3}, 13, 14\frac{1}{3}$

- The term to term rule can also be used to find missing terms.

Example

$13, 8, 3, \underline{\hspace{1cm}}, -7, \ldots$

The term to term rule is -5 and so the missing term is -2.

Quick Test

1. Write down the term to term rule for this sequence:
   $24, 12, 6, 3, 1.5 \ldots$
2. Which of these sequences is arithmetic?
   A) $4, 6, 9, 13, 18, \ldots$ **B)** $5, 9, 13, 17, 21, \ldots$
3. Find the missing term in the following sequence of numbers.
   $15, 9, 3, \underline{\hspace{1cm}}, -9, -15, \ldots$
4. Which of these sequences is geometric?
   A) $4, 8, 16, 32, 64, \ldots$ **B)** $16, 14, 12, 10, 8, \ldots$

Key Words

sequence
function machine
arithmetic sequence
geometric sequence
double
term to term

Algebra

Sequences 2

You must be able to:

- Generate the terms of a sequence from a position to term rule
- Find the *n*th term of an arithmetic sequence
- Recognise quadratic sequences.

The *n*th Term

- The **_n_th term** is also called the **position to term** rule.
- The *n*th term is an algebraic expression which represents the operations carried out by a function machine.

INPUT   OUTPUT

INPUT		OUTPUT
1		9
2	$\times 4 \longrightarrow + 5$	13
3		17
n		**4*n* + 5**

> **Key Point**
>
> For the first term in the sequence, *n* always equals 1.

- The **_n_th term** can be used to generate the terms of a sequence.

Example

The *n*th term of a sequence is given by $3n + 5$.

To find the first term you substitute $n = 1$.

$3 \times 1 + 5 = 8$ 8 is the first term in the sequence

To find other terms you can **substitute** different values of *n*.

When *n* = 2	When *n* = 3	When *n* = 4
$3 \times 2 + 5 = 11$	$3 \times 3 + 5 = 14$	$3 \times 4 + 5 = 17$
11 is the second term in the sequence	14 is the third term in the sequence	17 is the fourth term in the sequence

The *n*th term $3n + 5$ produces the sequence of numbers:

8, 11, 14, 17, 20…

The rule can be used to find any term in the sequence. For example, to find the 50th term in the sequence substitute $n = 50$:

$3 \times 50 + 5 = 155$

Finding the nth Term

- To find the nth term look for a pattern in the sequence of numbers.

Example

The first five terms of a sequence are 7, 11, 15, 19, 23.

The term to term rule is +4 so the nth term starts with $4n$.

The difference between $4n$ and the output in each case is 3 so the final rule is $4n + 3$.

Input	× 4	Output
1	4	7
2	8	11
3	12	15
4	16	19
5	20	23
n	$4n$	$4n + 3$

Quadratic Sequences

- **Quadratic** sequences are based on square numbers.

Example

The first five terms of the sequence $2n^2 + 1$ are:
3, 9, 19, 33, 51,…

Key Point

Use BIDMAS when calculating terms in a sequence.

- Triangular numbers are produced from a quadratic sequence.
- There are many other sequences, for example the first five terms for n^3 are 1, 8, 27, 64, 125.
- A Fibonacci sequence is formed by adding the two previous terms together to find the next term: 1, 1, 2, 3, 5, 8, 13, 21, …

Honly

Quick Test

1. Write down the first five terms in the sequence $5n + 3$.
2. Write down the first five terms in the sequence $5n^2 - 1$.
3. a) Find the nth term for the following sequence of numbers:
   20, 16, 12, 8, 4,…
   b) Find the 50th term in this sequence.
4. What is the nth term also known as?

Key Words

nth term
position to term
substitute
quadratic

Review Questions

Key Stage 2: Key Concepts

1 Which of the following numbers is closer to 2000?

1996   2007

Explain how you know.   [2]

2 Calculate 476 − 231   [2]

3 Complete the table below by rounding each number to the nearest 1000.

	To nearest 1000
4587	
45698	
457658	
45669	

[2]

4 Write these in order starting with the smallest.

0.56   **55%** $\frac{27}{50}$ **0.6**   **0.63**   [3]

5 Amy is twice as old as Rashmi.

Rashmi is 3 years younger than John.

John is 25 years old.

How old is Amy?   [2]

6 Calculate 467 × 34   [3]

7 Calculate 156 ÷ 3   [2]

8 On the scale below draw an arrow to show 1.4 and 3.6:

[2]

Total Marks _____ / 18

1 A bottle holds 1 litre of fizzy drink. Macie pours four glasses for her friends. Each glass contains 200ml.

How much fizzy drink is left in the bottle? [3]

2 Below are five digit cards.

| 7 | 5 | 1 | 6 | 3 |

Choose two cards to make the following two-digit number numbers:

a) A square number [1]

b) A prime number [1]

c) A multiple of 6 [1]

d) A factor of 60 [1]

3 An equilateral triangle has a perimeter of 27cm.

What is the length of one of its sides? [2]

4 $\frac{2}{3}$ of a number is 22.

What is the number? [2]

5 Here is an isosceles triangle drawn inside a rectangle.

Find the value of x. [3]

6 S and T are two whole numbers.

$$S + T = 500$$

S is 100 greater than T.

Find the value of S and T. [2]

Total Marks _____ / 16

Practice Questions

Number

1 Jessa and Holly have been given the following question:

What is the value of $3 + 5 \times 4 + 7$?

Jessa thinks the answer is 30 and Holly thinks the answer is 39. Who is right? Explain your answer. [2]

2 A netball club is planning a trip. The club has 354 members and the cost of the trip is £12 per member.

a) Work out the total cost of the trip. [3]

They need coaches for the trip and each coach seats 52 people.

b) How many coaches do they need to book? [3]

c) How many spare seats will there be? [2]

3 Alicia wants to buy 15 hotdogs.

Dave's dogs	Harry's hotdogs
3 hotdogs £4.00	5 hotdogs £6.00

Is Dave's dogs or Harry's hotdogs cheaper? Show your working. [3]

4 Fill in the missing number.

$$2 - \boxed{} = 5$$

[1]

Total Marks _____ / 14

1 120 can be written in the form $2^p \times q \times r$ where p, q and r are prime numbers.

Find the value of each of p, q and r. [3]

2 x and y are two different prime numbers. Find the highest common factor of the two expressions x^3y and xy^3 [2]

Total Marks _____ / 5

Sequences

1 **a)** Find the *n*th term of this arithmetic sequence: 4, 7, 10, 13, 16,... [3]

b) Find the 60th term in the sequence. [1]

(MR) **2** Match the cards on the left with a card on the right.

5, 9, 13, 17, 21...	Neither
2, 8, 18, 32, 50...	Quadratic
8, 17, 32, 53, 80...	Arithmetic

[2]

(MR) **3** **a)** Explain why $\sqrt{79}$ must be between 8 and 9. [2]

b) Use your calculator to find the value of $\sqrt{79}$ to 2 decimal places. [1]

Total Marks .... / 9

1 Match the sequence of numbers with the correct *n*th term.

2, 7, 12, 17, 22...	$5 - n$
3, 9, 27, 81...	$5n^2 + 1$
6, 21, 46, 81, 126...	$5n - 3$
4, 3, 2, 1, 0...	3^n

[2]

(PS) **2** The half-life of a radioactive material is the time taken for the level of radioactivity to decrease to half of its initial level.

A radioactive material is found which has a half-life of 1 day. The initial level in the sample taken was 800 units.

Find the amount of radioactive material left in the sample at the end of the 5th day. [2]

Total Marks .... / 4

Perimeter and Area 1

You must be able to:

- Find the perimeter and area of a rectangle
- Find the area of a triangle
- Find the area and perimeter of compound shapes.

Perimeter and Area of Rectangles

- The **perimeter** is the distance around the outside of a 2D shape.
- The formula for the perimeter of a rectangle is:

    perimeter = 2(length + width) or $P = 2(l + w)$

    also   perimeter = 2(length) + 2(width)

length (l)

width (w)

- The formula for the **area** of a rectangle is:

    area = length × width or $A = l \times w$

Example

Find the perimeter and area of this rectangle.

8 cm

3 cm

$$\begin{aligned} \text{Perimeter} &= 2(8 + 3) \\ &= 2 \times 11 \\ &= 22\text{cm} \\ \text{Area} &= 8 \times 3 \\ &= 24\text{cm}^2 \end{aligned}$$

Area of a Triangle

- The formula for the area of a triangle is:

    area = $\frac{1}{2}$(base × **perpendicular** height)

Example

Find the area of the following triangle.

3 cm

6 cm

$$\begin{aligned} \text{Area} &= \frac{1}{2}(6 \times 3) \\ &= \frac{1}{2}(18) \\ &= 9\text{cm}^2 \end{aligned}$$

Key Point

When finding the area of a triangle, always use the perpendicular height.

Area and Perimeter of Compound Shapes

- A **compound** shape is made up from other, simpler shapes.
- To find the area of a compound shape, divide it into basic shapes.

$$5 \times 7 - (4 \times 4)$$
$$35 - 16 = 19$$

Example

This shape can be broken up into three rectangles.

The areas of the individual rectangles are 2cm², 2cm² and 12cm².

The area of the compound shape is $2 + 2 + 12 = 16\text{cm}^2$.

> **Key Point**
>
> Areas are two-dimensional and are measured in square units, for example cm².

- To find the perimeter, start at one corner of the shape and travel around the outside, adding the lengths.

Example

Perimeter
$= 2 + 1 + 1 + 3 + 1 + 1 + 2 + 1 + 1 + 3 + 1 + 1$
$= 18\text{cm}$

> **Quick Test**
>
> 1. Find the perimeter of a rectangle with width 5cm and length 7cm.
> 2. Find the area of a rectangle with width 9cm and length 3cm. Give appropriate units in your answer.
> 3. Find the area of a triangle with base 4cm and perpendicular height 3cm.
> 4. Find the perimeter and area of this shape.
>
>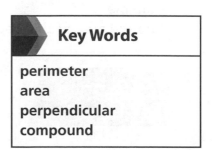

> **Key Words**
>
> perimeter
> area
> perpendicular
> compound

Perimeter and Area 2

You must be able to:

- Find the area of a parallelogram
- Find the area of a trapezium
- Find the circumference and area of a circle.

Area of a Parallelogram

- A **parallelogram** has two pairs of **parallel** sides.
- The formula for the area of a parallelogram is:
  area = base × perpendicular height

Example

Find the area of this parallelogram.

The base is 7cm and the perpendicular height is 3cm.

The area = $7 \times 3 = 21$cm^2.

Area of a Trapezium

- A **trapezium** has one pair of parallel sides.
- The formula for the area of a trapezium is $A = \frac{1}{2}(a + b)h$
- The sides labelled **a** and **b** are the **parallel** sides and **h** is the **perpendicular** height.
- This formula can be proved as follows:

- Two identical trapeziums fit together to make a parallelogram with base = $a + b$, height h and area $(a + b)h$.

Example

Find the area of this trapezium.

The area = $\frac{1}{2}(6 + 9) \times 4$
= 30cm^2

Circumference and Area of a Circle

- The radius of a circle is the distance from the centre to the **circumference**.
- The formula for the circumference of a circle is $C = 2\pi r$ or $C = \pi d$.
- The formula for the area of a circle is $A = \pi r^2$.

> **Key Point**
>
> The symbol π represents the number pi (3.141 592 654...).

Example

Find the circumference and area of a circle with radius 7cm.

Give your answers to 1 decimal place.

The circumference:

$C = 2 \times \pi \times 7$
$= 14 \times \pi$
$= 44.0\text{cm}$

The area:

$A = \pi \times 7^2$
$= 49 \times \pi$
$= 153.9\text{cm}^2$

- Circles can be split into **sectors**.
- Area of sectors can be calculated using fractions of 360°.

Example

Find the shaded region of a circle with radius 5cm when the angle at the centre is 30°.

The area of the whole circle is $\pi \times 5^2 = 25\pi$

The shaded sector is $\frac{30}{360}$th of the circle $= \frac{1}{12}$th

Area of sector $= \frac{25\pi}{12} = 6.5\text{cm}^2$ (1 d.p.)

> **Key Point**
>
> Arc length is the curved edge of a sector.

- Arc lengths can also be calculated using fractions of 360°. First, find the circumference of the circle, then multiply by the appropriate fraction of 360°.

> **Quick Test**
>
> 1. Find the area of the parallelogram.
>
>
>
> 2. Find the area of the trapezium.
>
>
>
> 3. Find the circumference and area of a circle with diameter 6cm.
> 4. Find the area of a sector with radius 4cm and angle 40° at the centre.

> **Key Words**
>
> parallelogram
> parallel
> trapezium
> circumference
> pi (π)
> sector

Statistics and Data 1

You must be able to:

- Find the mean, median, mode and range for a set of data
- Choose which average is the most appropriate to use in different situations
- Use a tally chart to collect data.

Mean, Median, Mode and Range

- The **mean** is the **sum** of all the values divided by the number of values.
- The **median** is the middle value when the data is in order.
- The **mode** is the most common value.
- The mean, median and mode are averages.
- The **range** is the **difference** between the biggest and the smallest value.
- The range is a measure of spread.

Key Point

Data can have more than one mode. Bi-modal means the data has two modes.

Example

Find the mean, median, mode and range for the following set of data:

5, 9, 7, 9, 2, 7, 3, 9, 4, 2, 6, 6, 4, 5

The mean $= \dfrac{5+9+7+9+2+7+3+9+4+2+6+6+4+5}{14}$

$= 5.6$ (to 1 d.p.)

The median = 2, 2, 3, 4, 4, 5, ⑤⑥ 6, 7, 7, 9, 9, 9

The median is the midpoint of 5 and 6 so 5.5

The mode is 9 as this number is seen most often.

The range $= 9 - 2 = 7$

Put the data in order, smallest to biggest.

Choosing which Average to Use

- Use the **mode** when you are interested in the most common answer, for example, if you were a shoe manufacturer deciding how many of each size to make.
- Use the **mean** when your data does not contain **outliers**. A company which wanted to find average sales across a year would want to use all values.
- Use the **median** when your data does contain outliers, for example finding the average salary for a company when the manager earns many times more than the other employees.

Key Point

An outlier is a value that is much higher or lower than the others.

Constructing a Tally Chart

- A tally **chart** is a quick way of recording data.
- Your data is already placed into groups, which makes it easier to analyse.
- A tally chart can be made into a **frequency** chart by adding an extra column to record the total in each group.

Example

You are collecting and recording data about people's favourite flavour crisps. You ask 50 people and fill in the tally chart as you ask each person.

Flavour	Tally	Frequency
Plain	卌 卌 ‖	12
Salt and vinegar	卌 ‖‖	9
Cheese and onion	卌 卌 卌	16
Prawn cocktail	卌 ‖	7
Other	卌	6

Quick Test

1. Emma surveyed her class to find out their favourite colour. She constructed this tally chart.
   a) Complete the frequency column.
   b) How many pupils are there in Emma's class?

Colour	Tally	Frequency
Red	卌 ‖‖	
Blue	卌 ‖	
Green	卌 ‖	
Yellow	卌	
Other	卌 ‖	

2. Look at this set of data:
   8, 7, 4, 6, 3, 5, 9, 40, 6
   a) Write down the mode.
   b) Calculate the mean, median and range.
   c) Would you choose the mean or the median to represent this data? Explain your answer.

Key Words

mean
sum
median
mode
range
difference
outlier
chart
frequency

Statistics and Data 2

You must be able to:

- Group data and construct grouped frequency tables
- Draw a stem-and-leaf diagram
- Construct and interpret a two-way table.

Grouping Data

- When you have a large amount of data it is sometimes appropriate to place it into groups.
- A group is also called a **class interval**.
- The disadvantage of using **grouped data** is that the original **raw data** is lost.

Example

The data below represents the number of people who visited the library each day over a 60-day period.

Number of people	Frequency
0–10	10
11–20	30
21–30	14
31–40	6

On 30 out of the 60 days the library had between 11 and 20, inclusive, visitors.

- To estimate the mean of grouped data the midpoint of each class is used.

Example

Calculate the mean of the data above.

Number of people	Midpoint (x)	Frequency (f)	fx
0–10	5	10	50
11–20	15.5	30	465
21–30	25.5	14	357
31–40	35.5	6	213
Total		60	1085

$$\frac{50 + 465 + 357 + 213}{60} = \frac{1085}{60}$$
$$= 18.1 \text{ (1 d.p.)}$$

Stem-and-Leaf Diagrams

- A stem-and-leaf diagram is a way of organising the data without losing the **raw data**.
- The data is split into two parts, for example tens and units.
- In this case the stem represents the tens and the leaves the units.
- Each row should be ordered from smallest to biggest.
- A stem-and-leaf diagram must have a **key**.

This is the number 1

KEY: 1|2 = 12

0	1 6 6 7 9
1	2 2 4 5 8 8 9
2	3 2 5 5 7
3	0 2

This is the number 32

> **Key Point**
>
> A stem-and-leaf diagram orders data from smallest to biggest.

Two-Way Tables

- A two-way table shows information that relates to two different categories.
- Two-way tables can be constructed from information collected in a survey.

Example

Zafir surveyed his class to find out if they owned any pets. In his class there are 16 boys and 18 girls. 10 of the boys owned a pet and 15 of the girls owned a pet.

	Pets	No Pets	Total
Boys	10	6	16
Girls	15	3	18
Total	25	9	34

The information given is filled into the table and then the missing information can be worked out.

> **Quick Test**
>
> 1. 25 women and 30 men were asked if they preferred football or rugby. 16 of the women said they prefer football and 10 of the men said they prefer rugby.
>   a) Construct a two-way table to represent this information.
>   b) How many in total said they prefer football?
>   c) How many women preferred rugby?
>   d) How many people took part in the survey?

> **Key Words**
>
> class interval
> grouped data
> raw data
> key

Number

(MR) **1** $48 \times 52 = 2496$

Use this to help you work out the following calculations:

$24 \times 52 =$ .... $48 \times$ .... $= 1248$ $2496 \div 52 =$ ....   [3]

(PS) **2** The lowest common multiple of two numbers is 60 and their sum is 27. What are the numbers?   [2]

(FS) **3** Gemma is having a barbecue and wants to invite some friends.

Sausages come in packs of 6. Rolls come in packs of 8. She needs exactly the same number of sausages and rolls.

What is the minimum number of each pack she can buy?   [3]

Total Marks .... / 8

1 Look at these expressions:

$45 = 5 \times 3^x$ $54 = 2 \times 3^y$

a) Find the values of x and y.   [2]

$45 \times 54 = 5 \times 2 \times 3^z$

b) Write down the value of z.   [1]

2 $25x^2$ must be a square number. Explain why.   [1]

(PS) **3** Two numbers have a sum of −5 and a product of 4. Write down the two numbers.   [1]

(MR) **4** Tom states that the sum of a square number and a cube number is always positive. Is he right? Give an example to justify your answer.   [2]

Total Marks .... / 7

Sequences

1 An expression for the nth term of the arithmetic sequence 6, 8, 10, 12,... is $2n + 4$.

   a) Find the 20th term of this sequence. [1]

   b) Find the 100th term of this sequence. [1]

2 The odd numbers form an arithmetic sequence with a common difference of 2.

   Find the nth term for the sequence of odd numbers. [2]

3 Lynne plants a new flower bush in her garden. Five of the buds have already flowered. Each week another three buds flower.

   a) How many buds will have flowered after three weeks? [1]

   b) How many weeks will it take for 32 buds to have flowered? [1]

   c) If n represents the number of weeks since Lynne planted her flower, write a rule to represent how many buds will flower after n weeks. [1]

                                                                          Total Marks _____ / 7

(MR) **1** The nth term for a sequence of numbers is $4n^2 + 2$.

   Wasim thinks the 10th term is 1602.

   Cindy thinks the 10th term is 402.

   Who is right?

   Explain your answer. [2]

2 Corinna visited the opticians to be fitted with some contact lenses. She is advised to wear them for three hours on the first day, and increase this by 20 minutes each day.

   After how many days will she be able to wear her contact lenses for 12 hours? [2]

                                                                          Total Marks _____ / 4

Practice Questions

Perimeter and Area

PS **1** The area of the rectangle shown is 48cm². [2]

Find the values of *X* and *Y*.

FS **2** Kelly is tiling a wall in her bathroom.

The wall is 4m by 3m. Each tile is 25cm by 25cm.

a) Work out how many tiles Kelly needs to buy for the wall. [3]

The tiles come in packs of 10 and each pack costs £15.

b) Work out how much it will cost Kelly to tile the wall. [2]

c) How many tiles will she have left over? [1]

Total Marks .... / 8

PS **1** The diagram shows a rhombus inside a rectangle.

The vertices of the rhombus are the midpoints of the sides of the rectangle.

Find the area of the rhombus. [3]

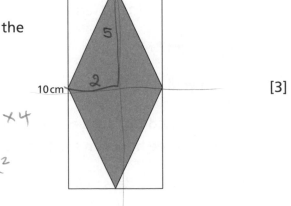

$$= \frac{1}{2}(5 \times 2) \times 4$$

$$= 20cm^2$$

Total Marks .... / 3

Statistics and Data

(MR) **1** Phil and Dave are good darts players.

They record their scores for a match. Their results are shown below.

	1	2	3	4	5	6	7	8	9
Phil	64	70	80	100	57	100	41	56	30
Dave	36	180	21	180	10	5	23	25	140

a) Calculate the mean score for each player. [2]

b) Find the range of scores for each player. [2]

c) One of the two players can be picked to play in the next match.

Would you pick Phil or Dave? Explain your answer. [2]

Total Marks _____ / 6

1 The grouped frequency table below gives details of the weekly rainfall in a town in Surrey over a year.

Weekly rainfall in mm	Number of weeks
$0 \leqslant d < 10$	20
$10 \leqslant d < 20$	18
$20 \leqslant d < 40$	10
$40 \leqslant d < 60$	4

Estimate the mean weekly rainfall. [3]

Total Marks _____ / 3

Decimals 1

You must be able to:

- Understand the powers of 10
- List decimals in size order
- Add, subtract and multiply decimals.

Powers of Ten

- A **power** or **index** tells us how many times a number should be multiplied by itself.

$10^2 = 10 \times 10$ $=$ 100

$10^3 = 10 \times 10 \times 10$ $=$ 1000

$10^4 = 10 \times 10 \times 10 \times 10$ $= 10\,000$

$10^{-1} = \dfrac{1}{10}$

$10^{-2} = \dfrac{1}{10^2} = \dfrac{1}{100}$

Ordering Decimals

- **Place value** can be used to compare decimal numbers.
- The numbers after the **decimal point** are called tenths, hundredths, thousandths, …

Example

Put these numbers in order from smallest to biggest:

12.071, 12.24, 12.905, 12.902, 12.061

Each number starts with 12. So compare the tenths, hundredths and thousandths.

	Tens	Units	.	Tenths	Hundredths	Thousandths
12.071	1	2	.	0	7	1
12.24	1	2	.	2	4	0
12.905	1	2	.	9	0	5
12.902	1	2	.	9	0	2
12.061	1	2	.	0	6	1

12.071, 12.061 are the two smallest as they have no tenths.

12.24 is the next smallest with 2 tenths.

12.905 and 12.902 are the two biggest as they have 9 tenths.

Next compare the hundredths and if needed the thousandths.

So from smallest to biggest:

12.061, 12.071, 12.24, 12.902, 12.905

Key Point

Ascending order is smallest to biggest; descending order is biggest to smallest.

Adding and Subtracting Decimals

- Decimal numbers can be added and subtracted in the same way as whole numbers.

Example

Calculate $23.764 + 12.987$

2	3	.	7	6	4
1	2	.	9	8	7

+

3	6	.	7	5	1
	1		1	1	

So $23.764 + 12.987 = 36.751$

Calculate $12.697 - 8.2$

$\cancel{1}$	$^1 2$	.	6	9	7
0	8	.	2	0	0

−

4	.	4	9	7

So $12.697 - 8.2 = 4.497$

Key Point

When adding and subtracting, line up the numbers by matching the decimal point.

Multiplying Decimals

- Complete the calculation without the decimal points and replace the decimal point at the end.
- Count how many numbers are after the decimal points in the question and this is how many numbers are after the decimal point in the answer.

Example

Calculate 45.3×3.7

$453 \times 37 = 16\,761$

There are two numbers after the decimal point in the question.

So $45.3 \times 3.7 = 167.61$

```
      5  4  †
         6  2
   ─────────
   1  0  8  2
3  2  4  6  0
───────────
3  3  5 , 4  2
```

Quick Test

1. Write down the value of 10^5.
2. Write the following numbers in ascending order:
   16.34, 16.713, 16.705, 16.309, 16.2
3. Work out $45.671 + 3.82$
4. Work out $34.321 - 17.11$
5. Work out 6.2×54.1

Key Words

power
index
place value
decimal point

Decimals 2

You must be able to:

- Divide decimal numbers
- Use rounding to estimate calculations
- Interpret and compare numbers in standard form.

Dividing Decimals

- **Equivalent** fractions can be used when dividing decimals.

Example

Calculate $4.45 \div 0.05$

$$4.45 \div 0.05 = \frac{4.45}{0.05} = \frac{445}{5} = 89$$

Remember to multiply the numerator and denominator by the same amount.

Rounding and Estimating

- Numbers can be rounded using **decimal places** or **significant figures**.

Key Point

Significant figures is often shortened to s.f.

Example

Round 56.76 to 1 decimal place.

56.$\underline{7}$|6

7 is the first decimal place and the number after it is more than 5, so round 7 up to 8.

56.76 rounded to 1 decimal place is 56.8

Example

Round 0.00764 to 2 significant figures.

0.007$\underline{6}$|4

6 is the second significant figure and the number after it is less than 5, so the 6 stays as a 6.

0.00764 rounded to 2 significant figures is 0.0076

Remember the first significant figure is the first non-zero digit.

- When **estimating** a calculation round all the numbers to one significant figure.

Example

$26\,751 \times 64$

An estimate for $26\,751 \times 64$ is $30\,000 \times 60 = 1\,800\,000$

- There is always a resulting error from approximations and estimates.

Example

$26\,751 \times 64 = 1\,712\,064$

An estimate for $26\,751 \times 64 = 1\,800\,000$

The resulting error is $1\,800\,000 - 1\,712\,064 = 87\,936$

- There is always an error to consider when a number is rounded.
- This error can be expressed using an inequality.

Example

A number has been rounded to 7.6 to 1 decimal place.
The diagram below shows the range of possible values the number could be.

7.5   7.6   7.7

       7.55   7.65

The number could be anywhere between 7.55 and 7.65, therefore the rounding error can be expressed as $-0.05 \leqslant \text{error} < 0.05$.

Standard Form

- **Standard form** is an easy way to write very big and very small numbers using powers of 10.
- A negative power means to divide, so $10^{-1} = \frac{1}{10}$

Example

2000 can be written as 2×1000, which is the same as 2×10^3.

0.0007 can be written as $7 \div 10\,000$, which is 7×10^{-4}.

- A number not written in standard form is called an **ordinary number**.

Example

Write 456 000 in standard form.

You can write this as $\boxed{4.56} \times 100\,000$, or 4.56×10^5 in standard form.

Write 0.00762 in standard form.

You can write this as $\boxed{7.62} \div 1000$, or 7.62×10^{-3} in standard form.

> **Key Point**
>
> When a number is written in standard form, the initial number must be between 1 and 10.

$1 \leqslant 4.56 < 10$

$1 \leqslant 7.62 < 10$

> **Key Words**
>
> equivalent
> decimal places
> significant figures
> estimate
> standard form
> ordinary number

> **Quick Test**
>
> 1. Work out $65.2 \div 0.4$
> 2. Estimate 3457×46
> 3. Write 569 000 in standard form.
> 4. Write 0.00087 in standard form.
> 5. Write 6.56×10^4 as an ordinary number.

Algebra 1

You must be able to:

- Know the difference between an equation and expression
- Collect like terms in an expression
- Write products as algebraic expressions
- Substitute numerical values into expressions.

Collecting Like Terms

- The difference between an **equation** and expression is that an equation has an equals sign.
- To **simplify** an **expression** like terms are collected together.

Example

Simplify $2x^2 + 6y - x^2 + 4y - 6$

Collect the like terms.

$$2x^2 - x^2 + 6y + 4y - 6$$

The x terms can be simplified: $2x^2 - x^2 = x^2$

The y terms can be simplified: $6y + 4y = 10y$

There is only one constant term.

So $2x^2 + 6y - x^2 + 4y - 6$ can be simplified to $x^2 + 10y - 6$

Example

Simplify $\frac{2}{3}x + 6y - \frac{1}{6}x + 4y$

Collect the like terms: $\frac{2}{3}x - \frac{1}{6}x + 6y + 4y$

The x terms can be simplified: $\frac{2}{3}x - \frac{1}{6}x = \frac{1}{2}x$

The y terms can be simplified: $6y + 4y = 10y$

So $\frac{2}{3}x + 6y - \frac{1}{6}x + 4y$ can be simplified to $\frac{1}{2}x + 10y$

Key Point

Remember the terms have a + or − sign between them and the sign on the left belongs to the term.

Expressions with Products

- **Product** means multiply.
- Expressions with products are written in shorthand.

Example

$2 \times a = 2a$

$a \times b = ab$

$a \times a \times b = a^2 b$

$a \div b = \dfrac{a}{b}$

$a \times a \times a = a^3$

Substitution

- A **formula** is a rule which links a variable to one or more other variables.
- The variables are written in shorthand by representing them with a letter.
- Substitution involves replacing the letters in a given formula or expression with numbers.

> **Example**
>
> Find the value of the expression $2a^3 + b$ when $a = 3$ and $b = 5$.
>
> Replace the letters with the given numbers.
>
> $2a^3 + b$
>
> $= 2 \times 3^3 + 5$
>
> $= 59$

- There are many scientific problems which involve substituting into formulae.
- Some commonly used scientific formulae are:

$$\text{speed} = \frac{\text{distance}}{\text{time}} \quad \text{in shorthand} \quad s = \frac{d}{t}$$

$$\text{density} = \frac{\text{mass}}{\text{volume}} \quad \text{in shorthand} \quad d = \frac{m}{v}$$

> **Example**
>
> Adriana's mum lives 30 miles from her house and on a particular morning last week her journey there took $\frac{3}{4}$ of an hour.
>
> Calculate her average speed in miles per hour.
>
> $s = \frac{d}{t}$
>
> $s = \frac{30}{0.75} = 40$mph

$\frac{3}{4} = 0.75$

- To find the area and volume of shapes, we substitute into a formula.
- Sometimes formulae need to be rearranged to solve a problem.
- Remember the following inverse operations:

Operation	Inverse
+	−
−	+
÷	×
×	÷

Key Words

equation
simplify
expression
product
formula

> **Quick Test**
>
> 1. Simplify $4x + 7y + 3x - 2y + 6$
> 2. Simplify $c \times c \times d \times d$
> 3. Find the value of $4x + 2y^2$ when $x = 2$ and $y = 3$

Algebra 2

You must be able to:

- Multiply a single term over a bracket
- Factorise linear expressions.

Expanding Brackets

- **Expanding** the brackets means remove the brackets by **multiplying** every term inside the bracket by the number or term on the outside.
- Take care over + and − signs. ≈ table in F
- Do not forget to simplify if possible.

Example

Expand and simplify $4(x + y) - 2(2x - 3y)$

×	4
x	$4x$
y	$4y$

$= 4x + 4y$

×	2
$2x$	$4x$
$-3y$	$-6y$

$= 4x - 6y$

Then collect like terms.

$(4x + 4y) - (4x - 6y) = 10y$

F & H

Example

Expand $2x^3(5x^2 - 6y^2)$

×	$2x^3$
$5x^2$	$10x^5$
$-6y^2$	$-12x^3y^2$

$2x^3(5x^2 - 6y^2) = 10x^5 - 12x^3y^2$

Higher Expanding
Two brackets
and brackets
with power

Key Point

Remember $x^m \times x^n = x^{m+n}$

Example

Expand $(x + 5)(x + 2)$

×	x	$+2$
x	x^2	$+2x$
$+5$	$+5x$	$+10$

$(x + 5)(x + 2) = x^2 + 7x + 10$

Key Point

When you multiply two brackets $(x + a)(x + b)$ you make four terms and then simplify.

Factorising

- **Factorising** is the opposite of expanding.
- When factorising we put the brackets back in.
- To factorise completely always take out the highest common factor.
- Always expand your answer to check you are right.

Example

Factorise $6x + 9$

3 is a common factor of 6 and 9 so we take the 3 to the outside of the bracket.

To find what is inside the bracket, we need to fill in the blanks in the table.

×	3
	$6x$
	$+9$

→

×	3
$2x$	$6x$
$+3$	$+9$

So $6x + 9 = 3(2x + 3)$

F & H

Example

Factorise $6x^3 + 2x^2$

Both 2 and x^2 are common factors.

×	$2x^2$
	$6x^3$
	$2x^2$

→

×	$2x^2$
$3x$	$6x^3$
$+1$	$2x^2$

So $6x^3 + 2x^2 = 2x^2(3x + 1)$

F & H

Example

Factorise $\frac{7}{9}xy + \frac{8}{9}y^2$

Both $\frac{1}{9}$ and y are common factors.

×	$\frac{1}{9}y$
	$\frac{7}{9}xy$
	$\frac{8}{9}y^2$

→

×	$\frac{1}{9}y$
$7x$	$\frac{7}{9}xy$
$8y$	$\frac{8}{9}y^2$

So $\frac{7}{9}xy + \frac{8}{9}y^2 = \frac{1}{9}y(7x + 8y)$

H *← fractions*

Quick Test

1. Expand $4(2x - 1)$
2. Expand and simplify $2(2x - y) - 2(x + 6y)$
3. Factorise $5x - 25$
4. Factorise completely $2x^5 - 4x^3$

So factorising powers of variable is F & H

Review Questions

Perimeter and Area

(FS) **1** Frances wants to paint the front of her house.
The diagram represents the front of Frances' house.

a) Find the area which Frances needs to paint. [3]

Each tin of paint covers 7m^2.

b) Work out the number of tins which Frances needs to buy. [1]

Each tin costs £12.

c) Work out how much it will cost Frances to paint the front of her house. [2]

(PS) **2** Yoon buys a new bicycle and uses it to cycle 8000m to work every day and then catches the train home. His wheel is a circle with a diameter of 50cm.

Work out how many times his wheel makes a full rotation during his journey. [2]

Total Marks _____ / 8

(MR) **1** a) Which of the two sectors below has the biggest area? Show working to justify your answer. [3]

Sector A   Sector B

Radius 3 cm   Radius 5 cm
$\frac{1}{5}$ of a circle $\frac{1}{9}$ of a circle

b) The perimeter is made up of two straight edges and the arc length.

Which of the two sectors above has the biggest perimeter?
Show working to justify your answer. [3]

Total Marks _____ / 6

Statistics and Data

PS **1** A midwife asked 60 of her patients if they wanted a home, hospital or water birth.

16 of her patients were teenagers.

10 of the teenagers wanted a hospital birth.

18 of the non-teenagers wanted a home birth.

4 of the 10 patients who wanted a water birth were teenagers.

How many patients wanted a hospital birth? [3]

MR **2** The data below shows the number of people attending the first six home matches for Sandex United football club:

   1240   1354   1306   14808   1378   1430

You want to calculate the average attendance.

Would you find the mean, median or mode? Give a reason for your answer. [1]

Total Marks _____ / 4

MR **1** Sophie carries out a survey to calculate the mean shoe size in her class. There are 28 pupils in her class. She calculates the mean to be 7.5

She thinks this is a little high, given her data, and decides to check her calculations. She realises she has used the value 40 instead of 4.

Calculate the correct mean. [3]

MR **2** Isabella is organising a charity netball event. She is planning on selling T-shirts to help raise extra money. She is trying to decide how many of each size T-shirt to order, so she does a survey of all the people in her class to find out their T-shirt size.

Should Isabella use the mean, median or mode as the average size in this case? Give a reason to justify your answer. [2]

Total Marks _____ / 5

Practice Questions

Decimals

1. Work out the following:

   a) $34.542 + 23.29$ [1]

   b) $65.21 - 43.23$ [1]

   c) 21.81×3.4 [1]

   d) $43.2 \div 0.2$ [1]

Total Marks _____ / 4

1. Join the pairs of cards that multiply to make 4.

0.02	0.08
50	0.2
8	200
20	0.5

   [2]

2. a) Write 6 890 000 in standard form. [1]

   b) Write 0.008 766 in standard form. [1]

   c) Which is larger, 5.989×10^4 or 59 890 000?
   Justify your answer. [1]

Total Marks _____ / 5

Algebra

(MR) 1 Chanda thinks the perimeter of the rectangle is $2x + 2y$.
Lawrence thinks the perimeter of the rectangle is $2(x + y)$.

Who is right? Chanda, Lawrence or both of them?
Explain your answer. [2]

(FS) 2 The cost (in £) of hiring a car for the day and driving it y miles is shown by this formula:

$$C = 75 + 0.4y$$

Work out how much it would cost to hire the car for a day and travel 120 miles. [3]

3 Expand and simplify $2(4x + 1) - 5(x - 1)$ [2]

4 Factorise completely $3abc + 6a$ [2]

(PS) 5 $ab = 36 \qquad a = 4$

Find the value of $a^2 b$ [2]

6 Complete the algebra grid alongside. Each brick is made by summing the two bricks underneath. [2]

Total Marks _____ / 13

---

1 Expand the brackets:

$(x + 4)(x - 2)$ [2]

2 Complete the following factorisations:

$x^2 + 3x + 2 = (x + 1)\,(\underline{} + \underline{})$

$x^2 + 5x - 6 = (x + 6)\,(\underline{} - \underline{})$ [2]

(MR) 3 Kathleen states that for all numbers $(x + y)^2 = x^2 + y^2$

Show that Kathleen is wrong. [2]

Total Marks _____ / 6

3D Shapes: Volume and Surface Area 1

You must be able to:

- Name and draw 3D shapes
- Draw the net of a cuboid and other 3D shapes
- Calculate the surface area and volume of a cuboid.

Naming and Drawing 3D Shapes

- A 3D shape can be described using the number of **faces**, **vertices** and **edges** it has.

Shape	Name	Edges	Vertices	Faces
	Cuboid	12	8	6
	Triangular prism	9	6	5
	Square-based pyramid	8	5	5
	Cylinder	2	0	3
	Pentagonal prism	15	10	7

> **Key Point**
>
> A face is a sur'face', for example a flat side of a cube.
>
> A vertex is where edges meet, for example a corner of a cube.
>
> An edge is where two faces join.

Using Nets to Construct 3D Shapes

- To create the **net** of a cuboid, imagine it is a box you are unfolding to lay it out flat.

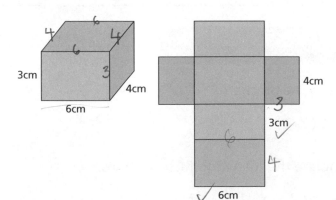

- Nets for a triangular prism and a square-based pyramid look like this:

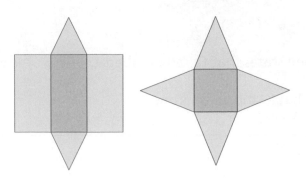

Surface Area of a Cuboid

- The **surface area** of a cuboid is the sum of the areas of all six faces and is measured in square units (cm^2, m^2, etc.).

Example

To calculate the surface area of the cuboid on the previous page, you can use the net to help you.

Work out the area of each rectangle by multiplying the base by its height:

Green rectangle: 6cm × 4cm = 24cm^2
There are two of them, so 24cm^2 × 2 = 48cm^2

Blue rectangle: 3cm × 6cm = 18cm^2
There are two of them, so 18cm^2 × 2 = 36cm^2

Pink rectangle: 4cm × 3cm = 12cm^2
There are two of them, so 12cm^2 × 2 = 24cm^2

Sum of all six areas 24 + 48 + 36 = 108cm^2

Volume of a Cuboid

- **Volume** is the space contained inside a 3D shape.

Example

To calculate the volume of the cuboid on page 42 you need to first work out the area of the front rectangle:
3cm × 6cm = 18cm^2

Next multiply this area by the depth of the cuboid, 4cm.

18cm^2 × 4cm = 72cm^3

← The units are cm^3 this time.

Quick Test

Work out the volume and the surface area of these cuboids.

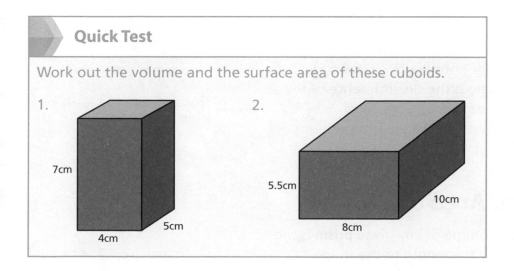

1. 7cm, 4cm, 5cm

2. 5.5cm, 8cm, 10cm

Key Words

face
vertex
edge
net
surface area
volume

3D Shapes: Volume and Surface Area 2

You must be able to:

- Calculate the volume and surface area of a cylinder
- Calculate the volume and surface area of a prism
- Calculate the volume of composite shapes.

Volume of a Cylinder

- You work out the volume of a **cylinder** the same way as the volume of a cuboid.
- First work out the area of the **circle** and then multiply it by the height of the cylinder.

Example
This cylinder has a **diameter** of 12cm.

So the **radius** is 6cm.

Volume $(\pi \times 6 \times 6) \times 5 = 565.49\text{cm}^3$ (2 d.p.)

Area of a circle = $\pi \times$ radius^2

Volume units are shown with a ^{3}, for example cm^3.

Surface Area of a Cylinder

- To calculate the surface area, first draw the net of a cylinder (imagine cutting a can open).

Example

Calculate the area of the circular ends $(\pi \times 3 \times 3) \times 2 = 56.55$ (2 d.p.) The area of the rectangle is the circumference of the circle multiplied by the height of the cylinder, 10cm.
$(\pi \times 6) \times 10 = 188.50$ (2 d.p.) Then add the areas together:
$56.55 + 188.50 = 245.05\text{cm}^2$

Because there are two circles!

Circumference = $\pi \times$ diameter
Diameter is double the radius.

Volume and Surface Area of a Prism

- In general we can say that the volume of any given **prism** is the cross-sectional area multiplied by the length of the shape.

Example

This is a triangular prism.
Work out the area of the triangle

$$(9 \times 12) \div 2 = 54cm^2$$

15cm
9cm
12cm
18cm

and multiply by the length.

$$54cm^2 \times 18cm = 972cm^3$$

For surface area, the triangular sides: $(9 \times 12) \div 2 = 54cm^2$
Two of these sides so $108cm^2$
The rectangular sides: $18 \times 12 = 216cm^2$ ✓
$18 \times 15 = 270cm^2$ ✓
$9 \times 18 = 162cm^2$ ✓

Total surface area $= 108 + 216 + 270 + 162 = 756cm^2$

Key Point

Finding the surface area of a triangular prism follows the same method as for the surface area of a cuboid. There are only two duplicate sides.

Volume of Composite Shapes

- A **composite** shape has been 'built' from more than one shape.

Example

This shape is built from two cuboids.

2cm
4cm
3cm
5cm
6cm

Calculate the volume of the two separate cuboids and add the volumes together.

$$(6cm - 2cm) \times 5 \times 3 = 60cm^3$$
$$(3cm + 4cm) \times 2 \times 5 = 70cm^3$$
$$60 + 70 = 130cm^3$$

Use the shape's dimensions to work out missing lengths.

Quick Test

1. Work out the volume and the surface area of these shapes to the nearest whole unit.

   a)
   8cm
   12cm

   b)
   10cm
   8cm
   5cm
   9cm

2. Work out the volume of this composite shape.

3cm
10cm
6cm
2cm
4cm

Handwritten: 3 x 6 x 2 + 10 x 2
x 4
36 + 280
116

Handwritten (right margin):
56. 54 866 776

188. 49 √ .

106 245.044

Key Words

cylinder
circle
diameter
radius
prism
composite

İnterpreting Data 1

You must be able to:

- Create a simple pie chart from a set of data
- Use and create a pictogram
- Draw a frequency diagram
- Make comparisons and contrasts between data.

Pie Charts

- **Pie charts** are often shown with **percentages** or **angles** indicating the sector size – this and the visual representation helps to **interpret** the data.

Example

36 students were asked the following question:

Which is your favourite flavour of crisps?

To work out the angle for each sector: 360 ÷ 36 = 10°

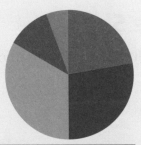

$$\frac{\text{Degrees in full turn}}{\text{Total}} = \text{Degrees per person}$$

Flavour of crisp	No. of students	Degrees
Salt and Vinegar ■	8	8 × 10 = 80
Cheese and Onion ■	10	10 × 10 = 100
Ready Salted ■	12	12 × 10 = 120
Prawn Cocktail ■	4	4 × 10 = 40
Other ■	2	2 × 10 = 20

> **Key Point**
>
> Always align your protractor's zero line with your starting line.
>
> Count up from zero to measure your angle.
>
> Don't forget to label your chart.

Pictograms

- Data is represented by a picture or symbol in a **pictogram**.

Example

The pictogram shows how many pizzas were delivered by Ben in one week. Key 🍕 = 8 pizzas

Day	Mon	Tue	Wed	Thu	Fri	Sat	Sun
Pizza deliveries	🍕🍕🍕	🍕	🍕◖	🍕	🍕🍕🍕🍕	🍕🍕	

How many pizzas did Ben deliver on Friday? 8 × 4 = 32

On Sunday Ben delivered 20 pizzas. Complete the pictogram.

20 ÷ 8 = 2.5 🍕🍕◖

Frequency Diagrams

- **Frequency** diagrams are used to show grouped **data**.

Example

The heights of 100 students are shown in this table.

Height in cm	70–80	81–90	91–100	101–110	111–120	121–130	131–140	141–150
Frequency	3	4	12	24	30	22	3	2

Using the span of each height category, plot each group as a block using the frequency **axis**.

Data Comparison

statistical

- You can make comparisons using ~~frequency~~ diagrams.

Example

This graph shows how much time two students spend on their mobile phones in a week. What does the graph show?

Apart from Thursday, Helen uses her phone more than Andy. Also, both of them use their phones more at the weekend.

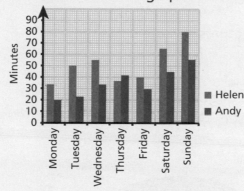

	M	T	W	Th	F	Sa	Su
H	34	50	55	36	40	65	80
A	20	23	34	42	30 / 45		55

diff | 14 | (27) | 21 | 6 | 10 | 20 | 25

Key Point

Think about what is similar about the data and what is different. Look for any patterns.

Quick Test

1. If 18 people were asked a question and you were to create a pie chart to represent your data, what angle would one person be worth?
2. Using the graph above, on which day did both Helen and Andy use their mobiles the most?
3. The following week Andy had a mean use of 40 minutes per day. Does this mean he uses his phone more than Helen now?

Key Words

pie chart
percentage
angle
interpret
pictogram
frequency
data
axis

Interpreting Data 2

You must be able to:

- Interpret different graphs and diagrams
- Draw a scatter graph and understand correlation
- Understand the use of statistical investigations.

Interpreting Graphs and Diagrams

- You can interpret the information in graphs and diagrams.

Example

What does this graph show?

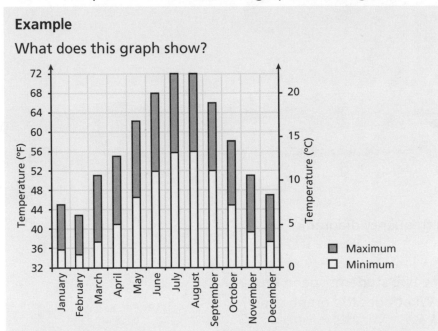

February has the lowest temperatures because it has the shortest yellow bar.

Use the labels and key to help.

Example

Using this pie chart, what is the most likely way the team scores a goal?

The largest sector of the pie chart here represents scoring a goal in free play.

Method of goals scored in the 2011 season – Mathletica E'Grid.

Own goals 2%
Penalties 10%
Corners 29%
Free play 39%
Free kicks 20%

Drawing a Scatter Graph

- A **scatter graph** shows two pieces of information on one graph.
- You can use a scatter graph to show a potential relationship between the data.
- You can draw a **line of best fit** through the points on a scatter graph.

Example

Here is a plot of the sales of ice cream against the amount of sun per day for 12 days. The scatter graph shows that when the weather is sunnier (and hotter) more ice creams are bought.

- You can describe the **correlation** and use the line of best fit to estimate data values.

- The graph above shows a positive correlation between ice cream sales and sunlight in a day.

- The graphs below show examples of negative correlation and no correlation.

Key Point

Plot each data pair as a coordinate.

A line of best fit doesn't have to start at zero or go exactly through any points.

Example

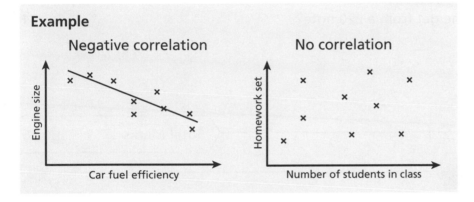

Statistical Investigations

- Statistical investigations use **surveys** and experiments to test statements and theories to see whether they might be true or false. We call these statements **hypotheses**.

Example

Jia needs to throw a 1 on a dice. She rolls it 25 times and still hasn't rolled a 1. What hypothesis might Jia make?

Hypothesis: The dice is biased.

You could test this hypothesis by rolling the dice a large number of times, determining whether it favours a certain number or not.

Quick Test

1. Look at the pie chart on page 48. What is the least likely way that Mathletica E'Grid scored a goal?
2. What correlation might you expect when comparing umbrella sales and rainfall?
3. Richard hasn't spun a yellow in 20 spins; his spinner has five different colours on it. What hypothesis might Richard suggest?

Key Words

scatter graph
line of best fit
correlation
survey
hypothesis

Review Questions

Decimals

1 Put the following numbers in order from smallest to biggest:

7.765, 7.675, 6.765, 7.756, 6.776 [2]

2 Tomas buys three books which cost £2.98, £3.47 and £9.54. 🔲

a) How much did the books cost in total? [2]

b) How much change did he get from a £20 note? [1]

Total Marks _____ / 5

FS **1** Louisa wants to buy some stationery. Here is a list of what she wants to buy:

Pencil 65p

Ruler £1.20

Pack of pens £4.99

Folder 98p

Eraser 48p

a) Find an estimate for the cost of her stationery. You should round all costs to 1 significant figure. [1]

b) Calculate the exact cost of her purchases. [1]

c) Find the percentage error in the estimate. [2]

Total Marks _____ / 4

Algebra

 1 This rectangle has dimensions $a \times b$

a) Write a simplified expression for the area of this rectangle. [1]

b) Write a simplified expression for the perimeter of this rectangle. [1]

c) Another rectangle has area $15a^2$ and perimeter $16a$. What are the dimensions of this rectangle? [1]

2 Look at this equation. $y = \dfrac{20}{\pm\sqrt{x + 10}}$

When $x = 90$ there are two possible answers. Write down both answers. [2]

3 Factorise the following expression completely: $8ut^2 - 4ut + 20t$ [2]

4 Kieran states 'If n is a positive integer then $4n$ will always be even'. Is Kieran correct? Explain your answer. [1]

Total Marks .... / 8

PS **1** a) Expand the expression $(x + y)(x - y)$ [1]

b) Use the expression $(x + y)(x - y)$ to find the answer to $201^2 - 199^2$. [2]

MR **2** Jack is buying a new desk for his bedroom. He chooses a desk but wants to check it will fit in the alcove in his bedroom. He measured the length of the desk to be 1.9m to the nearest centimetre. He measured his alcove to be 200cm to the nearest 10cm.

Desk 1.9m   Alcove 200cm

Will his desk definitely fit in the alcove? Justify your answer. [3]

Total Marks .... / 6

Practice Questions

3D Shapes: Volume and Surface Area

1 Calculate the surface area and volume of this cuboid. [2]

MR **2** Find the height of the cylinder with a radius of 5cm and volume of 942cm³. Give your answer to 1 decimal place. [2]

MR **3** Find the height of the cylinder with a radius of 7cm and volume of 1385cm³. Give your answer to 2 decimal places. [2]

Total Marks _____ / 6

MR **1** Calculate the surface area and volume of this triangular prism. [2]

MR **2** Find the volume of these shapes:

a) [6]

$14 \times 2 \times 2 + 8 \times 2 \times 2$

$= 22 \times 4 = 88$

b)

$14 \times 7 \times 4 - (2 \times 5 \times 4)$

$= 392 - 40$

$= 352 \, cm^3$

Total Marks _____ / 8

Interpreting Data

1 What two things might you plot against one another to show a negative correlation? [2]

2 Design a question with response box options to determine whether people shop more over the Christmas period than at other times of the year. [4]

(MR) **3** Name four different types of statistical graphs or charts. [4]

Which one would you use to plot the information collected from asking 40 students 'How long do you spend doing homework in a week?' Explain your choice. [4]

(MR) **4** The graphs below show the time spent talking on a mobile phone during one week for each couple.

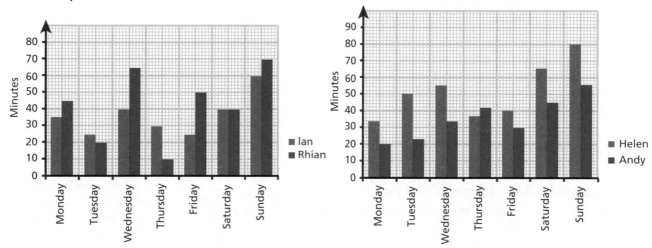

What comparisons can you make between the data?

Look at patterns between days of the week and differences between genders. [2]

Total Marks _____ / 12

1 Zarifa rolls an eight-sided dice more than 30 times and never rolls an 8.

What hypothesis might Zarifa suggest? How could she test her hypothesis? [3]

Total Marks _____ / 3

Fractions 1

You must be able to:

- Find and calculate equivalent fractions
- Add and subtract fractions.

Equivalent Fractions

- **Equivalent** fractions are fractions that are equal despite the denominators being different.

Example

$\frac{1}{2}$ $\frac{2}{4}=\frac{1}{2}$ $\frac{4}{8}=\frac{1}{2}$

- You can create an equivalent fraction by keeping the ratio between the **numerator** and **denominator** the same. You do this by multiplying or dividing both the numerator and denominator by the same number.

This is very useful when you want to compare or evaluate different fractions.

Example

Which is the larger fraction, $\frac{2}{5}$ or $\frac{3}{7}$?

To compare these fractions you need to find a common denominator, a number that appears in both the 5 and 7 times table.

$5 \times 7 = 35$

$\frac{2}{5}$ $\frac{3}{7}$

So $\frac{2}{5}$ becomes $\frac{14}{35}$ and $\frac{3}{7}$ can be $\frac{15}{35}$

Now the denominators are equal, you can evaluate the two fractions more easily.

You can see that $\frac{15}{35} = \frac{3}{7}$ is larger.

Key Point

A common denominator is a number that shares a relationship with both fractions' denominators.

For example, for 5 and 3 this would be 15, 30, 45, 60, …

Adding and Subtracting Fractions

- Adding fractions with the same denominator is straightforward. The 'tops', numerators, are collected together.

Example

$$\frac{1}{3} \quad + \quad \frac{1}{3} \quad = \quad \frac{2}{3}$$

 + =

The numerators are collected together.

Notice the size of the 'piece', the denominator, remains the same in both the question and the answer.

$$\frac{4}{5} \quad - \quad \frac{1}{5} \quad = \quad \frac{3}{5}$$

 – =

- When you have fractions with different denominators, first find equivalent fractions with a common denominator.

Example

$$\frac{1}{4} \quad + \quad \frac{2}{3} \quad = \quad \frac{3}{12} + \frac{8}{12} = \frac{11}{12}$$

 + =

Here the common denominator is 12, as it is the smallest number that appears in both the 3 and 4 times tables. This means that, for the first fraction you have to multiply both the numerator and denominator by 3 and for the second multiply by 4.

Now the fractions are of the 'same size pieces' you can add the numerators as before.

Quick Test

1. Find three equivalent fractions for $\frac{2}{3}$
2. $\frac{2}{7} + \frac{6}{11}$
3. $\frac{7}{9} - \frac{3}{8}$
4. $\frac{7}{13} - \frac{1}{4}$
5. $\frac{14}{25} + \frac{3}{5} - \frac{7}{20}$

Fractions 2

You must be able to:

- Multiply and divide fractions
- Understand mixed numbers and improper fractions
- Calculate sums involving mixed numbers.

Multiplying and Dividing Fractions

- Multiplying fractions by whole numbers isn't very different from multiplying whole numbers.
- The numerator is multiplied by the whole number.

> **Example**
>
> $\frac{2}{7} \times 3 = \frac{2}{7} + \frac{2}{7} + \frac{2}{7} = \frac{6}{7}$

- When multiplying fractions by fractions, you multiply the 'tops' and then multiply the 'bottoms'.

> **Example**
>
> $\frac{3}{5} \times \frac{2}{7} = \frac{3 \times 2}{5 \times 7} = \frac{6}{35}$
>
> When you multiply these two fractions, it is like saying there are $\frac{3}{5}$ lots of $\frac{2}{7}$.

- When dividing you use inverse operations. You change the operation to multiply and invert the second fraction.
- When you divide fractions you are saying how many of one of the fractions is in the other.

> **Example**
>
> $\frac{2}{5} \div \frac{1}{2} = \frac{2 \times 2}{5 \times 1} = \frac{4}{5}$
>
> $\frac{2}{5}$ divided into halves gives twice as many pieces.

Key Point

No common denominator is needed for multiplying or dividing fractions.

Mixed Numbers and Improper Fractions

- A **mixed number** is where there is both a whole number part and a fraction, for example $1\frac{1}{3}$.
- An **improper fraction** is where the numerator is bigger than the denominator, for example $\frac{4}{3}$.
- Improper fractions can be changed into a mixed number and vice versa.

Example

Changing an improper fraction to a mixed number:

$$\frac{14}{3} = 4\frac{2}{3}$$

> How many 3s are there in 14?

> The remainder is left as a fraction.

Changing a mixed number to an improper fraction:

$$4\frac{2}{3} = \frac{(4 \times 3) + 2}{3} = \frac{14}{3}$$

> Multiply the whole number by the denominator. 4 is 12 thirds

> Add the $\frac{2}{3}$ to make 14 thirds.

Adding and Subtracting Mixed Numbers

- To work with mixed numbers you first have to change them to improper fractions.
- There are four steps for addition:

  convert to improper fractions → convert to equivalent fractions → add → convert back to a mixed number.

  Example

  $$2\frac{4}{9} + 3\frac{1}{4} = \frac{22}{9} + \frac{13}{4} = \frac{22 \times 4}{36} + \frac{13 \times 9}{36} = \frac{205}{36} = 5\frac{25}{36}$$

- The same sequence of steps is needed for subtraction:

  convert to improper fractions → convert to equivalent fractions → subtract → convert back to a mixed number.

  Example

  $$4\frac{4}{7} - 1\frac{1}{4} = \frac{32}{7} - \frac{5}{4} = \frac{32 \times 4}{28} - \frac{5 \times 7}{28} = \frac{93}{28} = 3\frac{9}{28}$$

> **Key Point**
>
> Always write the 'remainder' as a fraction.

Quick Test

Work out:

1. $\frac{4}{5} \times \frac{5}{12}$

2. $\frac{7}{12} \div \frac{3}{7}$

3. $\frac{12}{15} \div \frac{5}{35}$

4. $5\frac{4}{7} + 3\frac{5}{6}$

> **Key Words**
>
> mixed number
> improper fraction

Coordinates and Graphs 1

You must be able to:

- Plot linear graphs
- Understand the components of $y = ax + b$
- Solve equations from linear graphs.

Linear Graphs

H — shows $x = -6$ & $y = -7$ but it's still F content (see Rac)

- **Coordinates** are usually given in the form (x, y) and they are used to find certain points on a graph with an x-**axis** and a y-axis.
- **Linear** graphs form a straight line.

Example

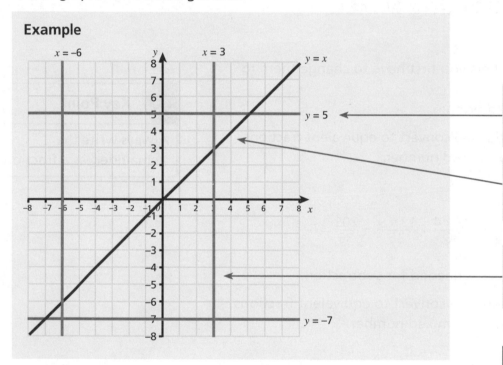

Plotting $y = 5$, we can choose any value for the x-coordinate but y must always equal 5. This line is parallel to the x-axis.

Plotting $y = x$, whatever x-coordinate you choose, the y-coordinate will be the same, e.g. (3, 3).

Plotting $x = 3$, we can choose any value for the y-coordinate but x must always equal 3. This line is parallel to the y-axis.

Graphs of $y = ax + b$

- a is used to represent the **gradient** of the graph.
- b is used to represent the **intercept**.
- To create the graph we substitute numbers for x and y.

Example

Plot the graph $y = 2x + 1$

If $x = 1$ you can work out what y is as follows:
$y = 2 \times 1 + 1 = 3$

Now change x to 2, 3, …

x	−1	0	1	2	3
y	−1	1	3	5	7

Key Point

A positive value of a will give a positive gradient. The graph will appear 'uphill'.

A negative value of a will give a negative gradient. The graph will appear 'downhill'.

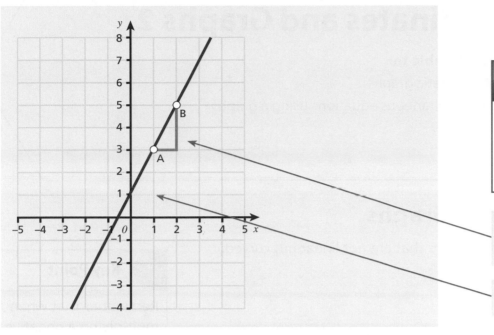

Key Point

Any value can be used for x to generate y, just try to pick one that is on your axes for ease.

When x increases by 1, y increases by 2.

$2 \div 1 = 2$ so the gradient is 2.

The line crosses the y-axis at 1 so the intercept is 1.

- You can work out the equation of a graph by looking at the gradient and the intercept.
- The gradient can be worked out by picking two points on the graph, finding the difference between the points on both the y- and x-axes and dividing them:

$$\frac{\text{difference in } y}{\text{difference in } x} = \text{gradient}$$

- The intercept is where the graph crosses the y-axis.

Solving Linear Equations from Graphs

- You can use a graph to find the solution to an equation.

Example

Using the graph $y = 2x + 1$ (above), you can find the solution to the equation $5 = 2x + 1$.

First of all plot the graph – see above. Then find where $y = 5$ on the axis.

Trace your finger across until it meets the graph and finally follow it down to read the x-axis value: $x = 2$

Quick Test

1. Complete the table below for the equation of $y = 3x - 4$, then plot it on a graph.

x	−2	−1	0	1	2	3
y						

2. If a graph has a gradient of 5 and an intercept of 3, what would the equation of this graph be?

Key Words

coordinates
axis
linear
gradient
intercept

Coordinates and Graphs 2

You must be able to:

- Plot quadratic graphs
- Solve simultaneous equations using a graph.

Drawing Quadratic Graphs

- **Quadratic equations** make graphs that are not linear but curved.

Example

$y = x^2$

Substitute values of x to create the coordinates.

x	−3	−2	−1	0	1	2	3
$y = x^2$	9	4	1	0	1	4	9

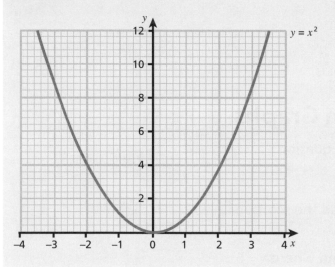

> **Key Point**
>
> Remember that when multiplying a negative with another negative, it becomes a positive number.

Because the equation $y = x^2$ has a power in it, this alters the graph to one that has a curve.

- Quadratics can take more complicated forms, but you still just **substitute** x for a number to get the coordinates.

Example

$y = x^2 + 2x + 1$

If $x = -3$ you can work out what y is as follows:

$y = (-3)^2 + 2(-3) + 1 = 9 + -6 + 1 = 4$

You can then work out the rest of the values of y by changing the value of x.

x	−3	−2	−1	0	1	2
y	4	1	0	1	4	9

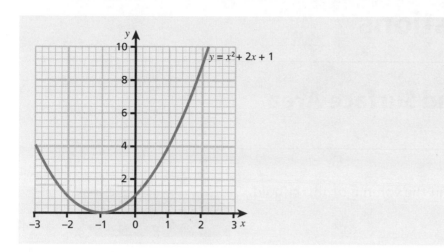

Solving Simultaneous Equations Graphically

- When you plot **simultaneous equations**, the solution to both equations can be seen at the point where both equations cross.

Key Point

Simultaneous equations are two equations that are linked.

Example

$y = x + 2$

$y = 8 - 2x$

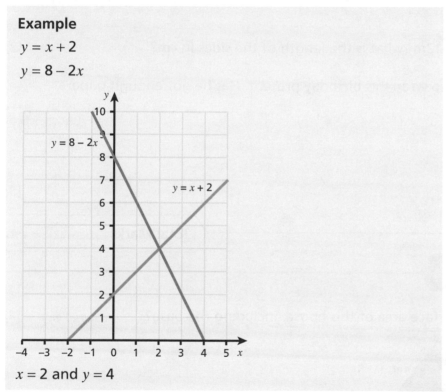

$x = 2$ and $y = 4$

Quick Test

1. What are the gradient and intercept of these equations?
   a) $y = 3x + 5$ b) $y = 6x - 7$ c) $y = -3x + 2$
2. Copy and complete the table for $y = x^2 + 3x + 4$

x	−3	−2	−1	0	1	2	3
y							

Key Words

quadratic equations
substitute
simultaneous equations

Review Questions

3D Shapes: Volume and Surface Area

1 Work out the surface area and the volume of this cuboid.

Do not forget the units.

[4]

2 Work out the volume of this oil drum to the nearest whole unit and state the units.

[3]

(MR) **3** If the volume of a cube is 512m³ what is the length of the sides in cm? [2]

(MR) **4** Phil has 1200cm² of paper to wrap this birthday present. Has he got enough paper? Show your working.

[3]

Total Marks _____ / 12

1 What is the volume and surface area of this house, including the base? [4]

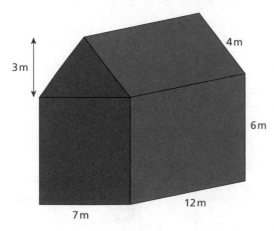

Total Marks _____ / 4

Interpreting Data

(MR) **1** Plot the following data on a graph.

Discuss any patterns, and what the graph shows.

TV viewing figures (in 1000s)	50	45	25	65	80	75	40	30	55
TV advert spend (in £1000s)	40	30	10	45	60	70	35	15	30

[4]

2 For each survey question below, state two things that could be improved.

a) Do you eat a lot of junk food? Yes ☐ No ☐ [2]

b) How much fruit do you eat in a week? 1 ☐ 2 ☐ 3 ☐ 4 ☐ [2]

Total Marks _____ / 8

1 Compare these two pie charts, which show how two people spend their spare time each week. [3]

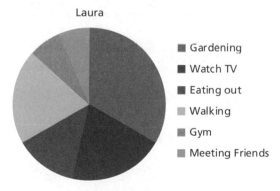

Laura

- Gardening
- Watch TV
- Eating out
- Walking
- Gym
- Meeting Friends

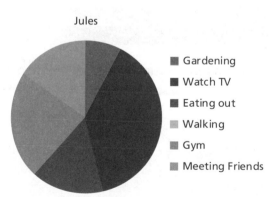

Jules

- Gardening
- Watch TV
- Eating out
- Walking
- Gym
- Meeting Friends

(MR) **2** Katya needs to spin a green to finish a game. After 12 goes she still hadn't done it. What hypothesis could Katya draw and how could she test it? [3]

Total Marks _____ / 6

Fractions

1 Solve and simplify:

    a) $\frac{4}{10} + \frac{1}{4} + \frac{2}{5} =$

    b) $\frac{2}{5} + \frac{1}{8} + \frac{1}{2} =$

    c) $\frac{3}{4} + \frac{2}{5} + \frac{3}{10} =$

    d) $\frac{3}{4} - \frac{1}{8} =$

    e) $\frac{5}{6} - \frac{1}{5} - \frac{1}{3} =$

    f) $\frac{7}{9} - \frac{1}{4} =$ [6]

2 Solve and simplify:

    a) $\frac{1}{8} \times \frac{2}{3} =$

    b) $\frac{5}{6} \times \frac{8}{9} =$

    c) $\frac{3}{10} \times \frac{1}{2} =$ [3]

3 Solve and simplify:

    a) $\frac{1}{8} \div \frac{2}{3} =$ [1]

    b) $\frac{1}{6} \div \frac{8}{9} =$ [2]

    c) $\frac{3}{4} \div \frac{3}{7} + \frac{1}{2} =$ [2]

Total Marks .... / 14

(MR) 1 Solve, giving your answer as a mixed number where appropriate.

    a) $4\frac{3}{8} + 2\frac{1}{5} =$ [2]

    b) $3\frac{3}{5} + 2\frac{3}{9} + 3\frac{1}{2} =$ [2]

    c) $7\frac{1}{4} - 2\frac{8}{11} =$ [2]

    d) $2\frac{1}{5} - 1\frac{3}{7} =$ [2]

Total Marks .... / 8

Coordinates and Graphs

(PS) 1 Find the missing coordinates when the points in this graph are reflected in the *y*-axis.

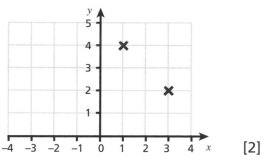

[2]

2 Draw the graph that shows the following lines:

a) $y = x$ b) $y = -x$ [2]

3 Using the equation below, complete the table and plot your results on a graph.

$y = -3x + 4$

x	−1	0	1	2	3
y					

[4]

Total Marks _____ / 8

1 What is the gradient and intercept of this graph?

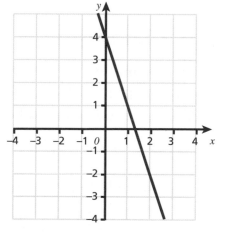

[2]

(MR) 2 Complete the table below for the quadratic equation $y = x^2 - 3x - 2$

x	−3	−2	−1	0	1	2	3
y							

[3]

Total Marks _____ / 5

Angles 1

You must be able to:

- Measure and draw angles
- Use properties in triangles to solve angle problems
- Use properties in quadrilaterals to solve angle problems
- Bisect an angle.

How to Measure and Draw an Angle

- **Angles** are measured in **degrees**, denoted by a little circle after the number, e.g. 45°.
- The piece of equipment used to measure and draw an angle is called a **protractor**.

Key Point

There are two scales on your protractor. This is so that the protractor can be used in two different directions.

Always start at zero and count up.

To measure the angle of a line:
- Place the protractor with the zero line on the base line.
- The centre should be level with the point where the two lines cross.
- Counting up from zero, count the degrees of the angle you are measuring.

To draw an angle:
- Draw a base line for the angle.
- Line up your protractor, putting the centre on the end of the line.
- Count up from zero until you reach your angle, e.g. 45°.
- Put a mark. Remove the protractor and draw a straight line joining the end of the base line to your point.

Angles in a Triangle

- Angles in any **triangle** add up to 180°.
- In an isosceles triangle, two (base) angles are the same.
- In a right-angled triangle, one angle is 90°.
- You can use these facts to help you work out missing angles.

Example

Find the missing angle x in these triangles.

$$180° - (90° + 35°) = x° = 55°$$

$$180° - (53° × 2) = x° = 74°$$

Angles in a Quadrilateral

- Angles in any **quadrilateral** add up to 360°.

Example

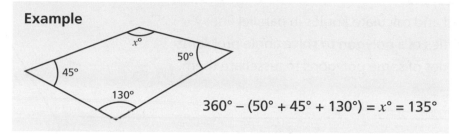

$$360° - (50° + 45° + 130°) = x° = 135°$$

- A parallelogram has two sets of equal angles. The opposite angles are equal.
- Only one angle is needed to be able to work out the others.

Example

$360° - (110° × 2) = 140°$
Now share this angle equally between the remaining two corners:
$x = 140° ÷ 2 = 70°$

Bisecting an Angle

- **Bisect** means to cut exactly into two.

Example
1. Open your compass to a distance that is at least halfway along one of the lines.
2. Put the point of the compass where the two lines touch. Mark an arc on both lines.
3. Now place the point on one of these arcs and draw another arc between the lines.
4. Repeat for the arc on the other line, creating a cross.
5. Draw a line from where the lines touch through the cross.

> **Quick Test**
>
> 1. Using a protractor draw an angle of:
>   a) 48°   b) 84°   c) 125°   d) 167°
> 2. Find the missing angle in each of these shapes.
>   a)   b)   c)
>
>

Key Words

angle
degree
protractor
triangle
quadrilateral
bisect

Angles 2

You must be able to:

- Understand and calculate angles in parallel lines
- Use properties of a polygon to solve angle problems
- Use properties of some polygons to tessellate them.

Angles in Parallel Lines

- **Parallel** lines are lines that run at the same angle.
- Using parallel lines and a line that crosses them, you can apply some observations to help find missing angles.
- The angles represented by ⚡ are equal. They are called **corresponding** angles.
- The angles represented by ♥ are also equal. They are called **alternate** angles.

- Alternate angles are also called Z angles, because the lines look like a Z.
- Corresponding angles are also called F angles, because the lines look like an F.

Angles in Polygons

- A **regular polygon** is a shape that has each of its sides and angles equal.
- Using the fact that angles in a triangle add up to 180°, you can split any shape into triangles to help you work out the number of degrees inside that shape.

> **Key Point**
>
> A polygon can be split into a number of triangles. Try this formula to speed up calculation:
>
> (No. of sides − 2) × 180 = sum of interior angles

- Dividing the total number of degrees inside a regular polygon by the number of vertices will give the size of one **interior angle**.
- The sum of the **exterior angles** of any shape always equals 360°.

Shape	Number of sides	Sum of the interior angles
Triangle	3	180°
Quadrilateral	4	360°
Pentagon	5	540°
Hexagon	6	720°
Heptagon	7	900°
Octagon	8	1080°

Example

The regular polygon has interior angles of 140°. How many sides does it have?

The exterior angle of each part of the polygon is 180° − 140° = 40°

360° ÷ 40° = 9, so the polygon has nine sides.

Polygons and Tessellation

- **Tessellation** is where you repeat a shape or a number of shapes so they fit without any overlaps or gaps.

Key Point

You may notice that shapes that tessellate have angles that add up to 360° about one point.

Quick Test

1. Find the missing angles:

2. Name two regular shapes that would tessellate.

Key Words

parallel
corresponding
alternate
regular polygon
interior angle
exterior angle
tessellation

Probability 1

You must be able to:

- Know and use words associated with probability
- Construct and use a probability scale
- Calculate the probability of an event not occurring
- Construct and use sample spaces.

Probability Words

- Certain words are used to describe the **probability** of an **event** happening. How would you describe:
  - The probability of there being 40 days in a month?
    Impossible – there are at most 31 days in a month.
  - The probability that a school student will attend school tomorrow?
    Likely – it cannot be said to be certain as the student might be on school holiday or ill and not attending school.
  - The probability that I roll a 2 on a dice?
    Unlikely – there are six possible outcomes and the number 2 is only one of these.
  - The probability that out of a bag with only green sweets in, a green sweet is pulled out?
    Certain – in this case there is no other outcome possible.
  - The probability a coin is thrown and it lands on heads?
    An **even chance** – the event outcome could be a head or a tail, two equally likely options.

> ### Key Point
>
> Try to consider the event with all the details. Do not just consider your own circumstance, it may be misleading!
>
> Once all the possible outcomes have been considered, the word can be selected.

Probability Scale

- A **probability scale** is a way of representing the probability words visually – putting the words we used above on a number line.
- The two extremes go at either end of the scale and the other probability words can be slotted in between:

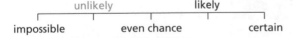

Example

Put an arrow on the probability scale above to represent the probability of pulling a red sweet out of a bag that contains 7 red sweets and 1 blue sweet.

- If an event has a more than equal outcome, then it is said to be **biased**.

Probability of an Event Not Occurring

- Probability can be thought of in terms of numbers as well as words. You could think of something happening as a fraction or a decimal.
- The probability of an event not happening can be summarised as 1 – event occurring.

Example

A non-biased six-sided dice is rolled:

P(rolling a 1) = $\frac{1}{6}$

P(rolling a 2) = $\frac{1}{6}$

P(rolling a 3) = $\frac{1}{6}$

P(rolling a 4) = $\frac{1}{6}$

P(rolling a 5) = $\frac{1}{6}$

P(rolling a 6) = $\frac{1}{6}$

P(not rolling a 4 or 5) = $1 - \left(\frac{1}{6} + \frac{1}{6}\right) = \frac{4}{6} = \frac{2}{3}$

Example

The probability of the weather being cloudy = 0.4

So the probability of it *not* being cloudy is 1 – 0.4 = 0.6

> **Key Point**
>
> When you add up all the possible event outcomes they should add up to 1.
>
> Use this fact to help you work out the probability of an event **not** occurring, by adding all the possible outcomes of the event occurring and taking them away from 1.

Sample Spaces

- A **sample space** shows all the possible outcomes of the event.

Example

The sample space for flipping a coin and rolling a dice is:

H1	H2	H3	H4	H5	H6
T1	T2	T3	T4	T5	T6

This shows all the possible outcomes and helps us to calculate the probability of events occurring.

> **Key Words**
>
> probability
> event
> impossible
> likely
> unlikely
> certain
> even chance
> probability scale
> biased
> sample space

Quick Test

1. How can the probability of rain in Manchester in October be described?
2. Show the event in question 1 on a probability scale.
3. A bag contains 5 red sweets and 10 blue sweets.
   a) What is the probability of picking a red sweet?
   b) What is the probability of not picking a red sweet?
4. If it rains 0.642 of the time in the rainforest and is cloudy 0.13 of the time, what is the probability it isn't raining or cloudy?

3dp

2dp

Probability 2

You must be able to:

- Understand what mutually exclusive events are
- Calculate a probability with and without a table
- Work with experimental probability
- Understand Venn diagrams and set notation.

Mutually Exclusive Events

- **Mutually exclusive** events can be defined as things that can't happen at the same time.
- For example, this spinner can't land on yellow and blue at the same time as it only has one pointer. You can say that the probability of getting a yellow and a blue is 0, i.e. mutually exclusive.
- You could calculate the probability of spinning a yellow or a blue, which would be $\frac{1}{4} + \frac{1}{4} = \frac{1}{2}$
- Wearing one orange sock and one purple sock would not be mutually exclusive as these events could happen at the same time.

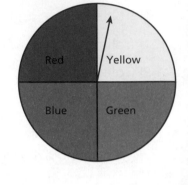

Calculating Probabilities and Tabulating Events

- Probability can be calculated by evaluating **all** outcomes.

> **Examples**
>
> What is the probability of picking a red ball from the bag?
>
> $\frac{7}{15}$
>
> The number of red balls / The total number of balls
>
> What is the probability of picking out a green *or* a blue ball?
>
> $\frac{3}{15} + \frac{4}{15} = \frac{7}{15}$

> There are three different colours in this bag of 15 balls: 3 yellow, some red and some blue balls. Use the table to work out the number of each colour ball.
>
> | Yellow | Red | Blue |
> |--------|-----|------|
> | 0.2 | 0.6 | ? |
>
> The probability that any ball is chosen is 1 so we can calculate the probability of drawing a blue ball: $1 - 0.6 - 0.2 = 0.2$
>
> One way of working out the actual number of each colour is to multiply the probability by the total number of balls:
> $15 \times 0.6 = 9$ (red) $0.2 \times 15 = 3$ (blue)

Experimental Probability

- The probability of getting a 6 when rolling a six-sided dice is $\frac{1}{6}$. If you rolled the dice six times would you definitely get a 6? You may not get a 6 in six rolls, however the more times you roll the dice the more likely you are to get closer to $\frac{1}{6}$. This is **experimental probability**.

Example

Hayley sat outside her school and counted 25 cars that went past. She noted the colour of each car in this table.

Yellow	1
Red	6
Blue	4
Black	9
White	5

a) What is the probability of the next car going past being white? $\frac{5}{25} = \frac{1}{5} = 0.2$

b) How many black cars would you expect if 50 cars go past? $\frac{9}{25} = 0.36$ $0.36 \times 50 = 18$

Venn Diagrams and Set Notation

- Venn diagrams can be used to organise sets and find probabilities.

Example

Set A is the children who like green beans. Set B is the children who like carrots.

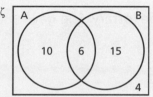

(A) = 10 + 6 = 16 children like green beans

(B) = 6 + 15 = 21 children like carrots

(A ∪ B) = 10 + 6 + 15 = 31 children like at least one. ← This is the union of A and B.

(A ∩ B) = 6 children like both green beans and carrots. ← This is the intersection of A and B.

(A ∪ B)′ = 4 children like neither green beans nor carrots. ← The symbol ' means not in A or B.

Quick Test

1. A bag has 20 balls of four different colours.
    a) Complete the table.

Yellow	?
Red	0.24
Green	0.19
Blue	0.1

    b) What is the probability of not getting a yellow ball?
    c) If I picked out and replaced a ball 50 times, what is the expected probability that I would pick out a green ball?

Fractions

1 Solve, giving your answers in their simplest form: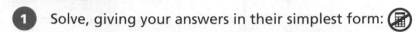

   a) $\frac{2}{5} + \frac{1}{10} =$ **b)** $\frac{7}{12} + \frac{1}{4} =$ **c)** $\frac{1}{6} + \frac{1}{5} =$

   d) $\frac{2}{7} + \frac{3}{10} =$ **e)** $\frac{8}{9} - \frac{1}{3} =$ **f)** $\frac{7}{11} - \frac{1}{2} =$

   g) $\frac{9}{10} - \frac{2}{3} =$ **[9]**

2 Solve, giving your answers in their simplest form:

   a) $\frac{4}{9} \times \frac{1}{5} =$ **b)** $\frac{3}{7} \times \frac{3}{10} =$ **c)** $\frac{5}{12} \times \frac{2}{3} =$

   d) $\frac{2}{9} \div \frac{1}{4} =$ **e)** $\frac{4}{5} \div \frac{6}{11} =$ **[7]**

(MR) 3 Sally won some money in the lottery. She gave $\frac{2}{5}$ to her husband and $\frac{1}{4}$ to her daughter.

   What fraction did she keep?   **[3]**

(MR) 4 Kamil was baking a cake. His recipe was $\frac{4}{9}$ flour, $\frac{1}{3}$ sugar and butter, and the rest an equal split of chocolate and eggs.

   What fraction does the chocolate part represent?   **[3]**

Total Marks _____ / 22

1 Change the following mixed numbers to improper fractions.

   a) $8\frac{5}{9}$ **b)** $3\frac{2}{7}$ **c)** $1\frac{3}{11}$ **[3]**

Total Marks _____ / 3

Coordinates and Graphs

1 Copy and complete the arrows and the table below, then plot the equation $y = 2x - 4$ on a graph.

```
⎡ × ⎤⟩  ⎡ − ⎤⟩
```

x	−1	0	1	2	3
y					

[4]

2 Copy and complete the table below for the equation $y = x^2 + 5x + 1$

x	−3	−2	−1	0	1	2	3
y							

[3]

Total Marks _____ / 7

 1 Will the graph $y = x^2 - 4x + 6$ have the coordinates (3, 3)? Justify your answer. [2]

 2 Find the solutions for the following simultaneous equations graphically.

$y = 4x + 2$

$y = -2x + 5$ [3]

 3 Match the equations with the same gradients:

a) $y = 2x + 12$

b) $y = 12 - 3x$

c) $y = 4x - 9$

d) $y = -3x + 5$

e) $2y = 4x + 2$

f) $y = 19 + 4x$ [3]

Total Marks _____ / 8

Practice Questions

Angles

1 Find the marked angle in this isosceles triangle.

[2]

PS **2** Find all the angles marked x and y indicated in each diagram.

a)

b)

[4]

3 What is the name of a polygon with 10 sides? [1]

PS **4** If each interior angle of a regular polygon is 150°, how many sides does it have? [2]

Total Marks .... / 9

1 Create a tessellation using at least six duplicates of these shapes.

 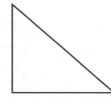

[3]

Total Marks .... / 3

Probability

1 Phil does an experiment dropping a paper cup a number of times. The probability of it landing upside-down is 0.65.

What is the probability of it NOT landing upside-down? [2]

(MR) 2 A dice has been rolled 50 times and recorded in the frequency table below.

a) Copy and complete the table. Give the probabilities as fractions. [3]

Number	Frequency	Estimated probability
1	5	
2	8	
3	7	
4	7	
5	8	
6	15	
Total		

b) Use the results in your table to work out the estimated probability (as fractions) of getting:

   i) the number 6   **ii)** an odd number   **iii)** a number bigger than 4 [3]

c) Do you think the dice is fair? Give a reason for your answer. [2]

Total Marks _____ / 10

1 Bradley has a pack of coloured cards. The table shows the probability of each colour being chosen.

Yellow	Red	Blue	Green	Pink
0.26	0.18	0.09		0.15

a) Copy and complete the table to show the probability of choosing a green card. [1]

b) What is the probability that a card is chosen and is not yellow? [2]

c) What is the probability that Bradley chooses a blue or green card? [1]

Total Marks _____ / 4

Fractions, Decimals and Percentages 1

You must be able to:

- Convert between a fraction, decimal and percentage
- Calculate a fraction of a quantity
- Calculate a percentage of a quantity
- Compare quantities using percentages.

Different Ways of Saying the Same Thing

- The table below shows how **fractions**, **decimals** and **percentages** are used to represent the same thing:

Picture	Fraction	Decimal	Percentage
$\frac{1}{4}$	$\frac{1}{4}$	0.25	25%
$\frac{1}{2}$	$\frac{1}{2}$	0.5	50%
$\frac{3}{4}$	$\frac{3}{4}$	0.75	75%

> **Key Point**
>
> **Percent** means 'out of 100'.

Converting Fractions to Decimals to Percentages

 Ave query

- For conversions you don't know automatically, use the rules below.

Fraction $\frac{1}{5}$

Put over 100 and cancel down $\left(\frac{20}{100}\right)$	↑		↓	Divide top by bottom ($1 \div 5$)

Decimal 0.2

$\div 100$ ($20 \div 100$)	↑			$\times 100$ (0.2×100)

Percentage 20%

Fractions of a Quantity

- To find a fraction of a **quantity** without a calculator, divide by the **denominator** and multiply by the **numerator**.

Example
Find $\frac{2}{3}$ of £120.

$$= 120 \div 3 \times 2 = £80$$

- To find a fraction of a quantity with a calculator, use the fraction button $\boxed{a^b/c}$. Calculators can differ though, so find out how yours deals with fractions.

Example
Find $\frac{2}{3}$ of £120.

$$= 2 \, \boxed{a^b/c} \, 3 \times 120 = £80$$

Percentages of a Quantity

- To find a percentage of a quantity without a calculator:

Example
Find 20% of $60.

$$10\% \text{ of } \$60 = 60 \div 10 = \$6$$
$$20\% = \$6 \times 2 = \$12$$

20% is 2 lots of 10%

- To find a percentage of a quantity with a calculator:

Example
Find 20% of $60.

$$= 20\% \times \$60$$
$$20 \div 100 \times 60 = \$12$$

OR 20% = 0.2
so 20% of $60 is
$0.2 \times \$60 = \$12$

Example
Find 120% of $60.

$$= 120\% \times \$60$$
$$= 120 \div 100 \times 60 = \$72$$

OR 120% = 1.2
so 120% of $60 is
$1.2 \times \$60 = \$72$

> **Key Point**
>
> Useful percentages to know:
>
> $50\% \rightarrow \div 2$
>
> $10\% \rightarrow \div 10$
>
> $1\% \rightarrow \div 100$
>
> 'of' means '$\times$'

Change the percentage to a decimal.

Remember: as 120% > 100%, your answer will be bigger than $60.

Comparing Quantities using Percentages

- To compare two quantities using percentages:

Example
Which is bigger, 30% of £600 or 25% of £700?

10% of £600 = 600 ÷ 10 = £60   50% of £700 = 700 ÷ 2 = £350
30% of £600 = 60 × 3 = £180   25% of £700 = 350 ÷ 2 = £175
30% of £600 is bigger, by £5.

> **Quick Test**
>
> 1. Change $\frac{7}{20}$ to a decimal and percentage.
> 2. Work out $\frac{2}{5}$ of £70.
> 3. Find 35% of £140.

> **Key Words**
>
> fraction
> decimal
> percentage
> quantity
> denominator
> numerator

Fractions, Decimals and Percentages 2

You must be able to:

- Work out a percentage increase or decrease
- Find one quantity as a percentage of another
- Work out simple interest
- Calculate a reverse percentage.

Percentage Increase and Decrease

- To find a percentage **increase** or **decrease**, add on or subtract the percentage you have found.

> **Example**
> A calculator is priced at £12 but there is a discount of 25%.
> Work out the reduced price of the calculator.
>
> $$25\% \text{ of } £12$$
> $$= 25\% \times £12$$
> $$= 25 \div 100 \times 12 = £3$$
>
> Reduced price = £12 − £3 = £9
> OR A reduction of 25% means you are left with 75%, and 75% = 0.75
> 0.75 × £12 = £9

£3 is the discount so **'take it away'** to get the final answer.

> **Example**
> A laptop computer costs £350 plus tax at 20%.
> Work out the actual cost of the laptop.
>
> $$20\% \text{ of } £350$$
> $$= 20\% \times £350$$
> $$= 20 \div 100 \times 350 = £70$$
>
> Actual cost = £350 + £70 = £420
> OR An increase of 20% means you pay 120%, and 120% = 1.2
> 1.2 × £350 = £420

£70 is the tax so **'add it on'** to get the final answer.

Finding One Quantity as a Percentage of Another

- To find one quantity as a percentage of another:

> **Example**
> Jane gets 18 out of 20 in a test. What percentage is this?
> **With a calculator:**
> $$\frac{18}{20} \times 100$$
> $$= 18 \div 20 \times 100$$
> $$= 90\%$$

Change the fraction to a decimal.

Without a calculator:

$$\frac{18}{20} \xrightarrow{\times 5} \frac{90}{100} = 90\%$$

$\times 5$ (below)

> Make the fraction 'out of' 100.

Simple Interest

- Find the **interest** for one year then multiply by the number of years.

Example

Alex puts £200 into a savings account. He gets 5% simple interest per year.

How much does he have in his account after two years?

$$10\% \text{ of } £200$$
$$= 200 \div 10$$
$$= £20$$
$$5\% = 20 \div 2 = £10$$

After two years Alex receives £10 × 2 = £20
Alex has £200 + £20 = £220 in his account.

> **Key Point**
>
> Interest is **not** added on at the end of each year.

> This is the interest for one year.

Reverse Percentages

- You are given the cost **after** the increase/decrease and will have to find the original cost.

Example

A car decreases in value by 20% to £5000. Find the original price of the car.

$$80\% = £5000$$
$$1\% = £5000 \div 80 = £62.50$$
$$100\% = £6250$$

The original price = £6250

> The **decrease** of 20% means that £5000 represents 80% of the original value.
>
> If it was an **increase** of 20% then you would write 120% = £5000

> **Quick Test**
>
> 1. A TV costing £450 is reduced by 10%. What is its sale price?
> 2. A house costing £80 000 increases in value by 15%. What is the cost of the house now?
> 3. Anna gets $\frac{21}{25}$ in a test. What percentage is this?
> 4. Write 24cm as a percentage of 30cm.
> 5. I save £400 at a simple interest of 5%. How much will I have after three years?
> 6. Find the original price of a house that has **increased** by 10% to £165 000.

> **Key Words**
>
> increase
> decrease
> interest

Equations 1

You must be able to:

- Solve a simple equation
- Solve an equation with unknowns on both sides
- Solve more complex equations
- Use negative numbers.

Solving Equations

- When you are asked to **solve** an **equation**, you need to find the value of the letter.
- Remember to think of the letter as 'something'.

Example

Solve the equation $2y + 3 = 15$

This simply means 'something' $+ 3 = 15$

so $2y = 12$

means $2 \times$ 'something' $= 12$

so $y = 6$

Now look with the **inverses**:

$$2y + 3 = 15$$

$(- 3)$ $2y = 12$

$(\div 2)$ $y = 6$

'Something' must be 12.

'Something' must be 6.

Key Point

Operation	Inverse
$+$	$-$
$-$	$+$
$\times$	$\div$
$\div$	$\times$

-3 is the 'inverse' or 'opposite' of $+3$.

$\div 2$ is the 'inverse' or 'opposite' of $\times 2$.

Equations with Unknowns on Both Sides

- An equation may have an unknown number on both sides of the equals sign.

Example

Solve the equation $5x - 2 = 3x + 5$

$$5x - 2 = 3x + 5$$

$(- 3x)$ $2x - 2 = 5$

$(+ 2)$ $2x = 7$

$(\div 2)$ $x = 3.5$

Get rid of all the xs on **one** side of the equation.

Remember to do the same to both sides.

Now do the inverses.

Solving More Complex Equations

- An equation may include a negative of the unknown number.
- The unknown number may be part of a fraction, or inside **brackets**.

Example

Solve the equation $3x + 1 = 11 - 2x$

$$3x + 1 = 11 - 2x$$

$(+ 2x)\quad 5x + 1 = 11$

$(- 1)\qquad 5x = 10$

$(\div 5)\qquad x = 2$

Be careful. This one has some negative xs.

Adding $2x$ to both sides gets rid of the negative xs.

Example

Solve the equation $\dfrac{3x + 1}{2} = 8$

$$\frac{3x + 1}{2} = 8$$

$(\times 2)\quad 3x + 1 = 16$

$(- 1)\qquad 3x = 15$

$(\div 3)\qquad x = 5$

Here, the $\times 2$ cancels out the $\div 2$ on the left-hand side of the equation.

Example

Solve the equation $3(2x - 1) = 4(x + 2)$

Multiply out the brackets first then solve in the usual way.

$$3(2x - 1) = 4(x + 2)$$

$$6x - 3 = 4x + 8$$

$(- 4x)\quad 2x - 3 = 8$

$(+ 3)\qquad 2x = 11$

$(\div 2)\qquad x = 5.5$

> **Key Point**
>
> Remember to multiply everything inside the bracket by the number outside the bracket.

Quick Test

1. If $6n = 30$, what is the value of n?
2. Solve the equation $3y - 2 = 13$
3. Solve the equation $3x + 7 = 2x - 2$
4. Solve the equation $2x + 1 = 13 - x$
5. Solve the equation $2(x + 2) = 2(3x - 2)$

Key Words

solve
equation
inverse
brackets

Equations 2

You must be able to:

- Set up and solve an equation
- Solve equations with x^2
- Use a method of trial and improvement.

Setting Up and Solving Equations

- You will have to follow a set of instructions in a given order.
- Usually you only have to $\times \div + -$ or square.
- If you have to multiply 'everything' then remember to use brackets.

Example

A number is doubled, then 5 is added to the total and the result is 11.

What was the original number?

The words	The algebra
A number	n
doubled	$2n$
add 5	$2n + 5$
The result is 11	$2n + 5 = 11$

You can now solve this in the usual way to find the original number equals 3.

Example

Three boys were paid £10 per hour plus a tip of £6 to wash some cars.

They shared the money and each got £12. How many hours did they wash cars for?

£10 × number of hours   £6 tip

Set up an equation: $\dfrac{10x + 6}{3} = 12$ each got

shared by 3 boys

Now solve the equation:

$$(\times 3) \quad 10x + 6 = 36$$
$$(- 6) \quad 10x = 30$$
$$(\div 10) \quad x = 3 \qquad \text{The boys worked for 3 hours.}$$

Key Point

Remember to do the same to both sides of the equation.

Equations Involving x^2

- Solving more complicated equations involving x^2 is usually done by the **trial and improvement** method.
- Try different values of x to get as close as you can to the answer.
- Find a value of x that gives an answer that is too big and one that is too small. Then try one that is in between.

> **Example**
>
> Solve the equation $x^2 + x = 15$. Give your answer to 1 decimal place.
>
> Try $x = 3$ $3^2 + 3 = 9 + 3 = 12$ ←   This is too small.
>
> Try $x = 4$ $4^2 + 4 = 16 + 4 = 20$ ←   This is too big.
>
> Now try a value between 3 and 4:
>
> Try $x = 3.5$ $3.5^2 + 3.5 = 12.25 + 3.5 = 15.75$ ←   This is too big.
>
> Try $x = 3.4$ $3.4^2 + 3.4 = 11.56 + 3.4 = 14.96$ ←   This is too small.
>
> Now try a value between 3.5 and 3.4:
>
> Try $x = 3.45$ $3.45^2 + 3.45 = 11.9025 + 3.45 = 15.3525$ ←   This is too big.
>
> The answer must be between 3.4 and 3.45 and therefore must **round** to 3.4 (1 d.p.)
> So, $x = 3.4$

- If you have to give your answer to 2 decimal places, you will need to show trials to 3 decimal places.

> **Key Point**
>
> Always make sure your trials are in order.
>
> Random tries will mean you do more work!

> **Quick Test**
>
> 1. A number is multiplied by 3 and then 8 subtracted from it. The result is 25. What is the number?
> 2. A chicken is roasted for 30 minutes for every kilogram plus an extra 20 minutes. If the chicken took 110 minutes to cook, how heavy was it?
> 3. Round 1.76 to 1 decimal place.
> 4. Solve the equation $x^2 = 5$
>   Give your answer to 1 decimal place.
> 5. Solve the equation $x^2 + 2x = 43$
>   Give your answer to 1 decimal place.

> **Key Words**
>
> trial and improvement
> rounding

Review Questions

Angles

1. Find the missing angles in the parallel line diagrams below.

   a)

   b)

   [4]

2. What do the total interior angles add up to in a nonagon? [1]

3. If each interior angle of a regular polygon is 160°, how many sides does it have?

   [3]

Total Marks _____ / 8

---

1. Explain why regular pentagons cannot be used on their own for tessellation.

   [3]

(MR) 2. Tessellate the following shape at least six times.

   [2]

Total Marks _____ / 5

Probability

1 Leanne runs an ice-cream van. At random, she chooses which kind of sprinkles to put on the ice-creams. The table below shows what Leanne did on Sunday.

Sprinkles	Frequency	Probability
Chocolate	19	
Hundreds and thousands	14	
Strawberry	7	
Nuts	10	

a) Complete the experimental probabilities in the table above. [2]

b) What was the probability of getting either nuts or chocolate sprinkles? [2]

2 If the probability of winning a raffle prize is 0.47, what is the probability of not winning a raffle prize? [1]

3 a) Complete the table below.

Sales destination	Probability of going to destination
London	0.26
Cardiff	0.15
Chester	0.2
Manchester	

[1]

b) Which is the least likely destination to travel to for sales? [1]

Total Marks _____ / 7

1 Yvonne works in insurance. The probability that Yvonne gets a claim from a call is 0.68

On Monday she gets 325 calls. What is the estimated number of claims? [2]

(MR) **2** Patrick is a baker. On Monday he made 250 bread rolls. However, Patrick's oven is slightly faulty and burns 0.14 of them. How many rolls were good on Monday? [2]

Total Marks _____ / 4

Practice Questions

Fractions, Decimals and Percentages

(PS) 1 Copy and complete the following table:

Fraction	Decimal	Percentage
$\frac{3}{5}$		
		55
	0.32	
$\frac{3}{100}$		

[4]

(PS) 2 Work out:

a) $\frac{2}{3}$ of $15 [2]

b) $\frac{3}{7}$ of $210 [2]

c) $\frac{4}{9}$ of $27 [2]

Total Marks .... / 10

(PS) 1 Work out:

a) 15% of 80cm [2]

b) 35% of 160m [3]

c) 5% of $70 [2]

(PS) 2 A jacket costing £75 is reduced by 20% in a sale. What is the sale price of the jacket? [3]

(FS) 3 Kim puts £300 into a savings account. She will receive 5% simple interest each year.

How much will she have in the bank after the following?

a) two years [3]

b) five years [3]

Total Marks .... / 16

Equations

(PS) **1** Solve these equations:

    a) $2x - 5 = 3$ [2]

    b) $3x + 1 = x + 7$ [2]

    c) $2(2x - 3) = x - 3$ [2]

    d) $\dfrac{3x + 5}{4} = 5$ [2]

(PS) **2** A number is multiplied by 3, then 2 is added to the total and the result is 11.

    What was the original number? [2]

3 At Anne's party there were 48 cans of drink. Everybody at the party had 4 cans each.

    How many people were at the party? [2]

    Total Marks .... / 12

(PS) **1** Solve the equation $3(x + 1) = 2 + 4(2 - x)$ [3]

2 Solve the equation $5(2a + 1) + 3(3a - 4) = 4(3a - 6)$ [3]

(PS) **3** A solution of $x^3 - x = 50$ lies between 3 and 4. Use a method of trial and improvement to find the value of x to 1 decimal place. [4]

4 Solve the equation $x^2 + 2x = 75$. Use a method of trial and improvement and give your answer to 1 decimal place. [4]

(MR) **5** The rectangle and the triangle have the same perimeter.

    Write down an equation and solve it to find the value of x. [4]

    Total Marks .... / 18

Symmetry and Enlargement 1

You must be able to:

- Reflect a shape
- Find the order of rotational symmetry
- Rotate a shape
- Translate a shape
- Enlarge a shape.

Reflection and Reflectional Symmetry

- Reflect each point one at a time.
- Use a line that is **perpendicular** to the mirror line.
- Make sure the **reflection** is the same distance from the mirror line as the original shape.
- A shape has reflectional symmetry if you can draw a mirror line through it.

Translation

- When a shape has shifted left/right (x) and/or up/down (y).
- The shift is given as a vector $\begin{pmatrix} x \\ y \end{pmatrix}$

Rotational Symmetry

- A shape has rotational symmetry if it looks exactly like the original shape when it is **rotated**.
- The 'order' of rotational symmetry is the number of ways the shape looks the same.
- To rotate a shape you need to know:
  - The **centre of rotation**
  - The direction it will rotate
  - The number of degrees to rotate.

order 1   order 2   order 3   order 4

Example

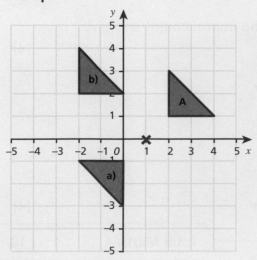

a) Rotate shape A 180° from (1, 0).

b) Translate shape A by vector $\begin{pmatrix} -4 \\ 1 \end{pmatrix}$.

Enlargement

- To draw an **enlargement** you need to know two things:
  - How much bigger/smaller to make the shape. This is called the **scale factor**.
  - Where you will enlarge the shape from. This is called the **centre of enlargement**.
- Remember: Enlarged shapes are **similar** (the same shape but a different size).

Example

Enlarge shape A by a scale factor of 2 from the point (3, 4).

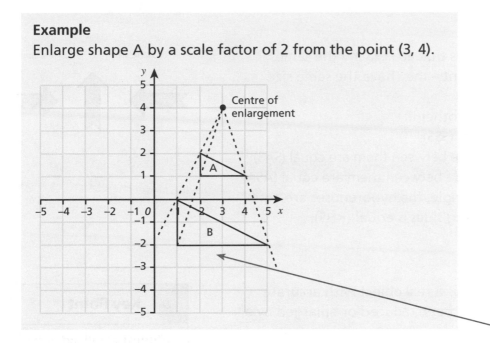

Enlarge every side of the shape.

- Use **rays** to check the position of your enlargement. They will touch corresponding corners of the shape.

Quick Test

1. What is the order of rotational symmetry of this shape?

2. a) Reflect this shape across the mirror line.
   b) Rotate the shape 180° about the corner A.

3. a) Rotate the shape in question 2 90° clockwise about the corner B.
   b) Enlarge this shape by a scale factor of 3.

1 cm
2 cm

Key Words

perpendicular
reflection
rotation
centre of rotation
enlargement
scale factor
centre of enlargement
similar
ray

Symmetry and Enlargement 2

You must be able to:

- Recognise congruent shapes
- Interpret a scale drawing
- Work out missing sides in similar shapes
- Convert between units of measure.

Congruence

- Congruence simply means shapes that are exactly the same.
- These arrow shapes are **congruent** – they have the same size and same shape.
- Triangles are congruent to each other if:
  - three pairs of sides are equal (SSS)
  - two pairs of sides and the angle between them are equal (SAS)
  - two pairs of angles and the side between them are equal (ASA)
  - both triangles have a right angle, the hypotenuses are equal and one pair of corresponding sides is equal (RHS).

Same size   Same shape

Scale Drawings

- A scale drawing is one that shows a real object with accurate dimensions, except they have all been reduced or enlarged by a certain amount (called the **scale**).
- Similar shapes are enlarged by the same scale factor, but the angles stay the same.

> **Key Point**
>
> Remember **all** sides must be multiplied by the same number.

> **Example**
> A scale of 1 : 10 means in the real world the object would be 10 times bigger than in the drawing.
>
>
>
> These horses are similar – same shape, different size.

- We use scale drawings to make copies of real objects.

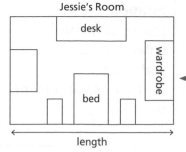

Jessie's Room

desk

wardrobe

bed

length

Scale: 1 inch = 3 feet

Here you would have to measure each side in inches then **multiply by 3** to get the real length in feet.

Shape and Ratio

- You can use ratios to work out the 'real' size of an object. The scale is given as a **ratio** with the smaller **unit** first.

Example
Estimate the height of this house using the scale of 1 : 160

5cm

6cm

> For every 1cm you measure in the picture, multiply by 160 to get the real size.
>
> Then convert to metres.

Here, the height of the house is 5cm so in real life the house is actually:

$5 \times 160 = 800cm = 8m$

The width of the house is 6cm so in real life the house is actually:

$6 \times 160 = 960cm = 9m\ 60cm$

Key Point

Scales are given as a ratio, usually 1 : n where n is what you multiply by.

Remember: 100cm = 1m

Quick Test

1. Draw three congruent shapes.
2. Which shape is congruent to shape A?

   A   B   C   D

3. Estimate the length, in metres of the boat. Scale: 1 : 80

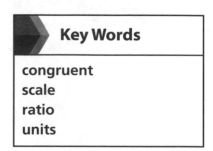

4. Which of these shapes are similar?

   2cm   4cm
   3cm   6cm   2cm   6cm
   A   B   C

5. Draw two shapes that are similar.

Key Words

congruent
scale
ratio
units

Ratio and Proportion 1

You must be able to:

- Understand what ratio means
- Simplify a ratio
- Multiply and divide by whole numbers.

Introduction to Ratios

- **Ratio** is a way of showing the relationship between two numbers.
- Ratios can be used to compare costs, weights and sizes.

> **Example**
>
> On the deck of a boat there are 2 women and 1 man. There are also 5 cars and 2 bicycles.
>
> The ratio of cars to bicycles is 5 to 2, written 5 : 2
>
> The ratio of bicycles to cars is 2 to 5, written 2 : 5
>
> The ratio of men to women is 1 to 2, written 1 : 2
>
> The ratio of women to men is 2 to 1, written 2 : 1

Key Point

'to' is replaced with ':'

- Ratios can also be written as fractions, for example: $\frac{2}{3}$ are women and $\frac{1}{3}$ are men, or $\frac{5}{7}$ of the vehicles are cars and $\frac{2}{7}$ of the vehicles are bicycles.

> **Example**
>
> A recipe for making pastry uses 4oz flour and 2oz butter.
>
> The ratio of flour to butter is 4 to 2, written 4 : 2
>
> The ratio of butter to flour is 2 to 4, written 2 : 4

> **Example**
>
> What is the ratio of black tiles to blue tiles?
>
>
>
> The ratio of black tiles to blue tiles is 5 : 9

Simplifying Ratios

- The following ratios are **equivalent**. The relationship between each pair of numbers is the same:

10 : 20

3 : 6

2 : 4

1 : 2   This ratio is a **simpler** way of writing the ratio 10 : 20

- You can **simplify** a ratio if you can divide by a common **factor**.
- When a ratio cannot be simplified, it is said to be in its **lowest terms**.

> **Key Point**
>
> When there are no more common factors, the ratio is in its lowest terms.

Example

Simplify the ratio 30 : 100

$30 \div 10$ 3 : 10 $100 \div 10$ ← Divide both numbers by 10.

Example

Write 40 cents to $1 as a ratio in its lowest terms.

First get the units the same: 40 cents to 100 cents written

40 : 100

Now simplify   ÷ 10   4 : 10

and again   ÷ 2   2 : 5   ← This is now in its lowest terms.

Example

The angles of a triangle are 20°, 60° and 100°.

What is the ratio of the angles in their lowest terms?

20° : 60° : 100°

(÷ 20) 1 : 3 : 5   ← This is now in its lowest terms.

Quick Test

1. Look at this pattern of grey and green tiles:

   a) Write down the ratio of green tiles to grey tiles.
   b) Write down the ratio of grey tiles to green tiles.
2. Write the following ratios in their lowest terms:
   a) 3 : 9   b) 28 : 4   c) 25cm : 1m

> **Key Words**
>
> ratio
> equivalent
> simplify
> factor
> lowest terms

Ratio and Proportion 2

You must be able to:

- Share in a given ratio
- Multiply and divide by whole numbers
- Work out proportional amounts
- Work out amounts that are inversely proportional.

Sharing Ratios

- Sharing ratios are used when a total amount is to be **shared** or **divided** into a given ratio.

Example

Share £200 in the ratio 5 : 3

Add together the ratio to find how many parts there are.

5 + 3 = 8 parts

Divide £200 by 8 to find out how much 1 part is.

200 ÷ 8 = 25

1 part is £25

Now multiply by each part of the ratio.

5 × £25 = £125

3 × £25 = £75

£200 shared in the ratio 5 : 3 is written £125 : £75

Key Point
Divide to find one, then multiply to find all.

Example

A sum of money is shared in the ratio 2 : 3

If the smaller share is £30, how much is the sum of money?

2 parts = £30

so 1 part = £30 ÷ 2 = £15

3 parts = £15 × 3 = £45

The sum of money = £30 + £45 = £75

Direct Proportion

- Two quantities are in **direct proportion** if their ratios stay the same as the quantities get larger or smaller.

> **Example**
> If the ratio of teachers to students in one class is 1 : 30, then three classes will need 3 : 90

Using the Unitary Method

- Using the unitary method, find the value of one unit of the quantity before working out the required amount.

> **Example**
> Five loaves of bread cost £4.25. How much will three loaves cost?
>
> One loaf costs £4.25 ÷ 5 = 85p
>
> Three loaves cost 85p × 3 = £2.55

Remember: divide to find one then multiply to find all.

Inverse Proportion

- Two quantities are in **inverse proportion** if one quantity increases as the other decreases.

> **Example**
> If six men build a wall in three days, how long will it take four men working at the same rate?
>
> Multiply to find one, then divide to find all.
>
> Six men take 3 days
>
> One man takes 3 × 6 = 18 days
>
> Four men take 18 ÷ 4 = 4.5 days

The reverse process to the one used in direct proportion.

One man will take longer to build the wall.

Four men will take $\frac{1}{4}$ of the time taken by one man.

> **Quick Test**
>
> 1. Share 40 sweets in the ratio 2 : 5 : 1
> 2. £360 is divided between Sara and John in the ratio 5 : 4 How much did each person receive?
> 3. Work out the missing ratio 4 : 5 = ? : 35
> 4. If six CDs cost £27, how much will eight CDs cost?
> 5. If it takes two men 6 days to paint a house, how long will it take three men painting at the same rate?

Key Words

share
divide
direct proportion
inverse proportion

Review Questions

Fractions, Decimals and Percentages

(PS) **1** a) Convert $\frac{13}{25}$ to a percentage. 🖹 [1]

b) Convert 0.375 to a fraction in its lowest terms. 🖹 [2]

c) Convert 36% to a fraction in its lowest terms. 🖹 [1]

(FS) **2** Seema receives £5 pocket money every week. She spends $\frac{1}{2}$ of her money on magazines and $\frac{2}{5}$ on sweets. The rest she saves.

a) How much does Seema spend on sweets? [2]

b) How much does Seema save? [2]

(PS) **3** Work out: 🖹

a) 20% of 300cm [2]

b) 6% of $140 [3]

c) 35% of 2800g [3]

(PS) **4** A coat costing £90 is reduced by 15% in a sale. What is the sale price of the coat? 🖹 [3]

(FS) **5** Karima puts £150 into a savings account. She will receive 6% simple interest each year.

How much will she have in the bank after the following:

a) 1 year [2]

b) 4 years [3]

Total Marks .... / 24

(MR) **1** Place the following numbers in order of size, starting with the smallest:

0.18 $\frac{3}{25}$ 16%   0.2 $\frac{7}{50}$ [2]

Total Marks .... / 2

Equations

(PS) **1** Solve these equations.

    a) $6x - 5 = 4x + 7$ [2]

    b) $5(x + 2) = 2(x - 1)$ [3]

    c) $3x - 1 = 4 - 2x$ [3]

    d) $\dfrac{6x - 5}{4} = 7$ [2]

2 A chocolate bar machine holds 56 bars of chocolate.

    If 29 are left, how many were sold? [2]

(FS) **3** Four builders are together paid £20 per hour plus a bonus of £150. They share the pay and each get £50.

    How many hours did they work? [3]

Total Marks _____ / 15

(PS) **1** Solve the equation $4(x - 2) - 2(3 - 2x) = 5x + 1$ [3]

> **Tip:**
> Expand the brackets first, collect like terms, then solve in the usual way.
> Remember:
> $- \times - = +$

2 Solve the equation $8 - 2a = 3(2a + 4)$ [3]

(PS) **3** A solution of $3x^2 - 2x = 70$ lies between 5 and 6.

    Use a method of trial and improvement to find the value of x to 1 decimal place. [4]

Total Marks _____ / 10

Symmetry and Enlargement

(PS) **1** Reflect shape A across the dotted mirror line.

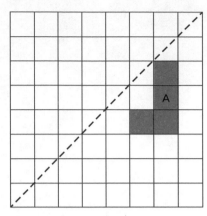

[2]

Total Marks .... / 2

(PS) **1** **a)** Rotate shape A 90° clockwise about the origin (0, 0). Label the new shape B. [2]

b) Enlarge shape A by a scale factor 3, with centre of enlargement (3, 4). Label the new shape C. [2]

c) Which of the shapes are congruent? [1]

d) Which of the shapes are similar? [1]

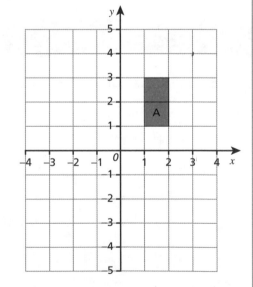

(MR) **2** A map is drawn on a scale of 1cm : 2km.

If a road is 13km long in real life, how long will it be, in cm, on the map? [2]

Total Marks .... / 8

Ratio and Proportion

PS ① What is the ratio of black tiles to white tiles? Give the ratio in its lowest terms. [1]

PS ② Simplify the following ratios:

a) 8 : 24 [1]

b) 40 minutes : 1.5 hours [2]

c) $3 : 80 cents [2]

FS ③ Ann, Ben and Cara share £480 in the ratio 4 : 5 : 3

How much does each person get? [3]

④ A sum of money is shared in the ratio 2 : 3

If the larger share is £27, how much money is there altogether? [3]

Total Marks _____ / 12

PS ① A recipe for 6 cupcakes needs 40g of butter and 100g of flour.

How much butter and flour is needed to make 15 cupcakes? [2]

PS ② Eight men can build a garage in 10 days. Working at the same rate, how long would it take:

a) 10 men? [2]

b) 5 men? [2]

Total Marks _____ / 6

Real-Life Graphs and Rates 1

You must be able to:

- Read values from a real-life graph
- Read a time graph
- Draw a graph of exponential growth.

Graphs from the Real World

- Graphs from the real world include **conversion graphs**.
- You may be asked to convert between these units:

  £ and $ £ and euros   pints and litres
  mph and km/h   miles and km   gallons and litres

Reading a Conversion Graph

- To convert from one unit to the other, read straight across to the line then go straight down until you reach the other axis. If you are converting the other way, go up until you reach the line, then read across.

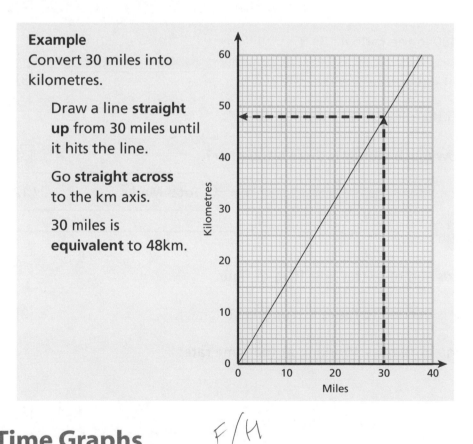

Example
Convert 30 miles into kilometres.

Draw a line **straight up** from 30 miles until it hits the line.

Go **straight across** to the km axis.

30 miles is **equivalent** to 48km.

> **Key Point**
>
> To go from kilometres to miles, read straight across to the line then go straight down until you hit the miles axis.

Time Graphs

F/H

- Distance–time graphs give information about journeys. Use the horizontal scale for time and the vertical scale for distance.
- Distance–time graphs are also used to calculate speeds.

Example

Amanda cycles to the gym and back every Sunday. The graph below shows Amanda's journey.

Amanda leaves the gym at 1.40pm and cycles home.

She takes 30 minutes.

Her speed on the return journey is 24km/h.

Amanda leaves home at 11.20am and cycles 12km in one hour.

Her speed is 12km/h.

Amanda arrives at the gym at 12.20pm and stays for one hour and 20 minutes.

Graphs of Exponential Growth

- **Exponential** growth means that the rate of growth is slow at the start and increases rapidly until it becomes massive.

H only

Example

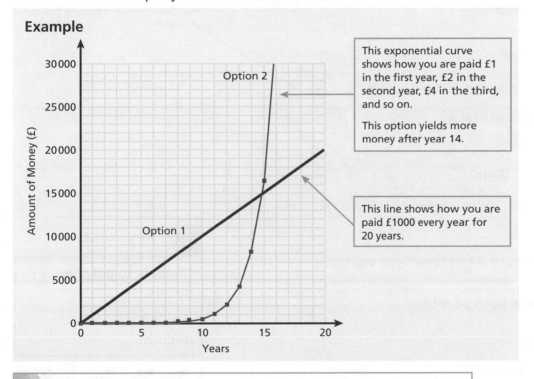

Option 2

Option 1

This exponential curve shows how you are paid £1 in the first year, £2 in the second year, £4 in the third, and so on.

This option yields more money after year 14.

This line shows how you are paid £1000 every year for 20 years.

Quick Test

Use the miles/km conversion graph on the previous page.
1. Find how many km are equivalent to: **a)** 25 miles **b)** 10 miles
2. Find how many miles are equivalent to: **a)** 30km **b)** 40km
3. Sharon charges £1 for the use of her taxi and 50 pence per mile after that. Work out the cost of a journey that is:
    a) 4 miles **b)** 6 miles long

Key Words

conversion
graph
exponential

Real-Life Graphs and Rates 2

You must be able to:

- Work out speeds, distances and times
- Work out unit prices
- Work out density.

Travelling at a Constant Speed

- When the speed you are travelling at does not change, it remains **constant**.
- You can work out a **speed, distance** or time using the formula triangle.

> **Example**
> A car travels 120 miles at 40 miles per hour.
> How long does it take?
>
> time = distance ÷ speed
>
> time = 120 ÷ 40 = 3 hours

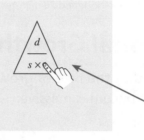

Cover up what you are trying to find.

> **Example**
> A plane takes $2\frac{1}{2}$ hours to travel 750 miles.
>
> What is the speed of the plane?
>
> speed = distance ÷ time
>
> speed = 750 ÷ 2.5 = 300mph

Unit Pricing

- **Unit** pricing simply means use what 'one' is to work out other amounts.
- This is often used in conversions of money.

> **Example**
> £1 = $1.75
>
> How much would a pair of jeans cost in $ if they were £60?
>
> 60 × 1.75 = $105
>
> How much would a TV costing $525 be in £?
>
> 525 ÷ 1.75 = £300

Key Point

Multiply to get the dollars.

Divide to get the pounds.

Density

- **Density** uses a formula triangle like speed.

density = mass ÷ volume

Example

Find the density of an object that has a mass of 60g and a volume of 25cm³.

density = mass ÷ volume

= 60 ÷ 25

= 2.4g/cm³

Example

The volume of a gold bar is 100cm³.

The density of gold is 19.3g/cm³.

Work out the mass of the gold bar.

mass = density × volume

mass = 19.3 × 100

= 1930g or 1.93kg

Cover up what you are trying to find.

Example

Calculate the volume of a piece of metal that has a mass of 2000kg and a density of 4000kg/m³.

volume = mass ÷ density

volume = 2000 ÷ 4000

= 0.5m³

Key Point

Remember to use the correct units.

Volume: **cm³, m³**

Mass: **g, kg**

Density: **g/cm³, kg/m³**

Quick Test

1. What is 90 minutes in hours?
2. Stuart drives 180km in 2 hours 15 minutes. Work out Stuart's average speed.
3. John travelled 30km in $1\frac{1}{2}$ hours.
   Kamala travelled 42km in 2 hours.
   Who had the greater average speed?
4. If £1 = €1.2, what would £200 be worth in €?
5. What is the mass of 250ml of water with density of 1g/cm³?

Key Words

constant
speed
distance
unit
density

Right-Angled Triangles 1

You must be able to:

- Label right-angled triangles correctly
- Know Pythagoras' Theorem
- Find the length of the longest side
- Find the length of a shorter side.

Pythagoras' Theorem

- Remember the formula for **Pythagoras' Theorem**: $a^2 + b^2 = c^2$

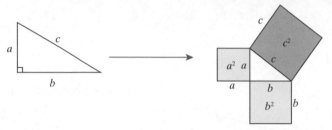

> **Key Point**
>
> The longest side, the hypotenuse, is called c and is opposite the right angle.
>
> The two shorter sides are a and b in any order.

Finding the Longest Side

- To find the longest side **(hypotenuse)**, **add** the **squares**. Then take the **square root** of your answer.

Example

Find the length of y. Give your answer to 1 decimal place.

Label the sides a, b and c first.

Now use the formula:

$$a^2 + b^2 = c^2$$

$$13^2 + 4.1^2 = y^2$$

$$169 + 16.81 = y^2$$

$$185.81 = y^2$$

$$y = \sqrt{185.81}$$

$$= 13.6\text{cm (1 d.p.)}$$

Finding a Shorter Side

- To find a shorter side, **subtract** the squares. Then take the square root of your answer.

Example

Find the length of y. Give your answer to 1 decimal place.

Label the sides a, b and c.

Now use the formula:

$a^2 + b^2 = c^2$

$7^2 + y^2 = 14^2$

$49 + y^2 = 196$

$y^2 = 196 - 49 = 147$

$y = \sqrt{147} = 12.1$cm (1 d.p.)

Example

Find the length of y. Give your answer to 1 decimal place.

Label the sides a, b and c.

Now use the formula:

$a^2 + b^2 = c^2$

$4^2 + y^2 = 15^2$

$16 + y^2 = 225$

$y^2 = 225 - 16 = 209$

$y = \sqrt{209} = 14.5$cm (1 d.p.)

> ### Key Point
> You will always $\sqrt{}$ at the end.

Quick Test

1. Work out:
   a) 3.2^2
   b) 15.65^2
2. Work out:
   a) $\sqrt{4900}$
   b) $\sqrt{39.69}$
3. Work out the longest side of a right-angled triangle if the shorter sides are 5cm and 2.2cm.
4. Work out the shorter side of a right-angled triangle if the longest side is 12cm and one of the other shorter sides is 9cm.

Key Words

Pythagoras' Theorem
hypotenuse
square
square root

Right-Angled Triangles 2

You must be able to:

- Remember the three ratios
- Work out the size of an angle
- Work out the length of a missing side.

Side Ratios

- Label the sides of the triangle in relation to the angle that is marked.

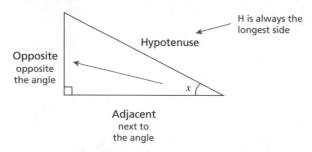

H is always the longest side

Hypotenuse

Opposite
opposite the angle

Adjacent
next to the angle

x

- There are three ratios: **sin, cos** and **tan**. Try to find a way of remembering these:

$$\sin x° = \frac{O}{H} \qquad \cos x° = \frac{A}{H} \qquad \tan x° = \frac{O}{A}$$

  - You can use the formula triangles:

  - You can use a rhyme:
    Some Old Horses Can Always Hear Their Owners Approach

Example

Use your calculator to work out the ratios for these angles:

a) sin 60° = 0.8660
b) cos 45° = 0.7071
c) tan 87° = 19.0811

Example

Use your calculator to work out the angle for these ratios:

a) $\sin x° = 0.5$ $\quad x = \sin^{-1} 0.5 = 30°$

b) $\cos x° = \frac{3}{5}$ $\quad x = \cos^{-1}(3 \div 5) = 53.1°$

c) $\tan x° = 2.9$ $\quad x = \tan^{-1} 2.9 = 71°$

Key Point

Ensure your calculator is in '**degree**' mode.

Finding Angles in Right-Angled Triangles

- You need to know two sides of the triangle to find an angle.

Example

Find the size of angle x. Give your answer to 1 decimal place.

As **A** and **H** are left we will use the cos ratio.

$$\cos x° = \frac{3.2}{7} \qquad x = \cos^{-1}(3.2 \div 7) = 62.8°$$

Key Point

The inverse of cos is $\cos^{-1}$.

Finding the Length of a Side

- You need to know the length of one side and an angle.

Example

Find the length of the side labelled y. Give your answer to 1 decimal place.

As **O** and **H** are left we will use the sin ratio.

$$\sin 63° \times 7 = y \qquad y = 6.2\text{m}$$

Quick Test

1. Use your calculator to work out the ratios for these angles:
   a) sin 20° b) cos 30° c) tan 45°
2. Use your calculator to work out the angles for these ratios:
   a) $\sin x° = 0.8337$ b) $\cos x° = \frac{4}{7}$ c) $\tan x° = 32$

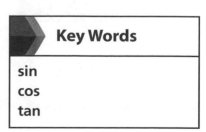

Key Words

sin
cos
tan

Review Questions

Symmetry and Enlargement

PS **1** Reflect shape A across the dotted mirror line.

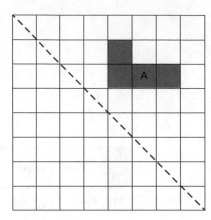

[2]

Total Marks _____ / 2

PS **1** a) Rotate shape A 180° about the point (2, 2).
Label the new shape B. [2]

b) Enlarge shape A by a scale factor of 2, with centre
of enlargement (2, 3). Label the new shape C. [2]

c) What is the area of shape A? [1]

d) What is the area of the shape C? [1]

e) What is the ratio of the areas A : C? [1]

MR **2** Find the width of the enlarged photograph. [2]

9 cm

6.4 cm

11.25 cm

x cm

Total Marks _____ / 9

Ratio and Proportion

(PS) **1** Simplify the following ratios.

    a) 16 : 24   [1]

    b) 25 cents : $2   [2]

    c) 0.75km : 200m   [2]

2 Work out the missing ratio.

    a) 8 : 3 = ? : 15   [1]

    b) 7 : ? = 63 : 108   [1]

    c) 4 : 5 = 6 : ?   [1]

3 Share 40 pens in the ratio 3 : 5   [2]

(FS) **4** A sum of money is shared in the ratio 1 : 4 : 3

    If the largest share is £120, how much money is there altogether?   [3]

Total Marks _____ / 13

(PS) **1** A machine can produce 1140 plastic cups in 8 hours. At the same rate, how many plastic cups can be made in:

    a) 10 hours?   [2]

    b) 12 hours?   [2]

(PS) **2** If it takes two men 3 days to paint a room, how long would it take three men to paint the same room?   [2]

(MR) **3** Twelve bags of oats will be enough for three donkeys for eight days.

    How long will 10 bags last four donkeys if they are given the same amount each day?   [3]

Total Marks _____ / 9

Real-Life Graphs and Rates

(FS) **1** Each year, there is a tennis competition in Australia and another one in France. The table shows how much money was paid to the winner of the men's competition in each country in 2012.

Country	Australia	France
Money	1 000 000 Australian dollars (£1 = 2.70 Australian dollars)	780 000 euros (£1 = 1.54 euros)

Which country paid more money? You must show your working. [2]

(PS) **2** The graph shows the flight details of an aeroplane travelling from London to Madrid via Brussels.

What is the aeroplane's average speed from London to Brussels?

[2]

Total Marks _____ / 4

(PS) **1** a) Calculate the density of a piece of metal that has a mass of 2000kg and a volume of 0.5m³. [2]

b) Calculate the volume of the same type of metal that has a mass of 5000kg. [2]

Total Marks _____ / 4

Right-Angled Triangles

(PS) **1** Use Pythagoras' Theorem to work out:

a) The length of BC

b) The length of AC

[4]

(PS) **2** **a)** Work out the value of p.

b) Work out the size of angle y.

[4]

Total Marks _____ / 8

(PS) **1** Work out the value of angle x.

$\cos x = \dfrac{8}{20}$

$x = 66.4°$

[3]

(MR) **2** State whether or not each triangle is right-angled.

a) 7cm, 12cm, 18cm

b) 10cm, 24cm, 26cm

c) 11cm, 19cm, 21cm

d) 7cm, 24cm, 25cm

[4]

Total Marks _____ / 7

Review Questions

Real-Life Graphs and Rates

FS **1** Use £1 = US$1.75 to work out how much:

a) US$200 is in £ [2]

b) £200 is in US$ [2]

PS **2** A coach travels 300 miles at an average speed of 40mph.

a) For how many hours does the coach travel? [2]

b) At the same speed how far will the coach travel in four hours? [2]

Total Marks _____ / 8

PS **1** At time $t = 0$ one bacteria is placed in a dish in a laboratory. The number of bacteria doubles every 10 minutes.

a) Draw a graph to show the growth of bacteria over 100 minutes. [3]

b) Use your graph to estimate the time taken to grow 300 bacteria. [1]

Time (t minutes)	No. of bacteria
0	1
10	
20	
30	
40	
50	
60	
70	
80	
90	
100	

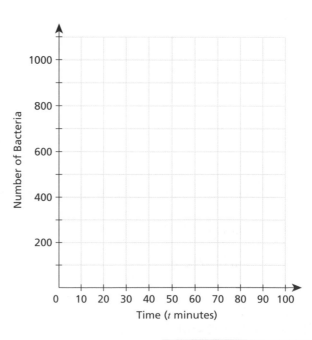

Total Marks _____ / 4

Right-Angled Triangles

1 **a)** Work out the value of angle x.

b) Work out the length of x.

[4]

2 **a)** Work out the length of y.

b) Work out the length of AB.

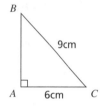

[4]

3 A wire 18m long runs from the top of a pole to the ground as shown in the diagram. The wire makes an angle of 35° with the ground.

Calculate the height of the pole. Give your answer to a suitable degree of accuracy.

[2]

Total Marks _____ / 10

1 **a)** Work out the vertical height of triangle ABC.

[2]

b) Work out the value of angle x.

[2]

Total Marks _____ / 4

No Calculator Allowed 🖩

1 Work out both the surface area and volume of each of these cuboids.

a)

2cm
4cm
6cm

Surface area = _____ cm²

Volume = _____ cm³

b)

7cm
12cm
8cm

Surface area = _____ cm²

Volume = _____ cm³

4 marks

2 Solve the following putting your answer in the simplest form.

a) $4\frac{1}{2} + 2\frac{1}{3} =$

b) $5\frac{2}{3} + 8\frac{1}{4} =$

c) $9\frac{1}{6} - 2\frac{3}{8} =$

d) $12\frac{1}{2} - 14\frac{5}{6} =$

4 marks

3 **a)** Plot the following coordinates onto the graph below: (3, 5) (1, 5) (2, 7)

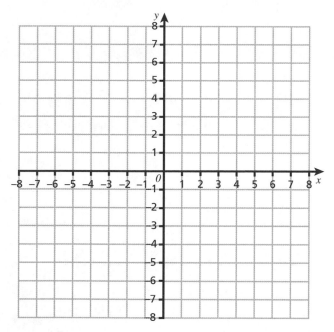

b) The three points are points on a rhombus. What is the fourth point?

2 marks

4 **a)** Complete the table below for the equation of $y = -2x + 3$

x	−2	−1	0	1	2	3
y						

b) Plot the coordinates on the graph below and join them with a line.

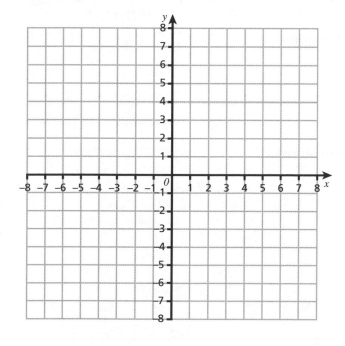

4 marks

TOTAL

14

5 Calculate angles x and y.

a)

$x =$ _____ °

$y =$ _____ °

b)

$x =$ _____ °

$y =$ _____ °

4 marks

6 **a)** Simplify the following expressions:

i) $3x - 2y + x + 6y$

ii) $4g + 5 - g - 4$

b) Expand and simplify the following expressions:

i) $4(x - 5)$

ii) $4x(x + 4)$

c) Factorise completely the following expressions:

i) $6x - 12$

ii) $4x^2 - 8x$

6 marks

7 The rectangle and trapezium below have the same area.

Work out the value of Z. Show your working.

3 marks

8 **a)** Two numbers have a sum of –5 and a product of 6.

Work out the two numbers.

b) Two different numbers have a sum of 7 and a product of –8.

Work out the two numbers.

2 marks

TOTAL

15

9 The shape below is made from four congruent triangles like the one on the right.

a) Write an expression in terms of a, b and c for the perimeter of the shape.

b) Given that $a = 3$, $b = 4$ and $c = 5$ find the value of the perimeter.

4 marks

10 A certain plant grows by 10% of its height each day. At 8am on Monday the plant was 400mm high.

How tall was it:

a) at 8am on Tuesday?

b) at 8am on Wednesday?

2 marks

11 **a)** Solve the equation $3y - 2 = 13$

b) Solve the equation $3 - \frac{x}{4} = -5$

4 marks

12

a) Reflect shape A in the y-axis.

b) Enlarge shape A by a scale factor of 2 from the point (3, 4).

c) Rotate shape A 180° from (0, 0)

3 marks

TOTAL

13

Calculator Allowed

1 Sam sat on the dock of a bay watching ships for an hour. He collected the following information:

Type	Frequency	Probability
tug boat	12	
ferry boat	2	
sail boat	16	
speed boat	10	

a) Complete the table's probability column, giving your answers as fractions.

b) If Sam saw another 75 boats, estimate how many of them would be sail boats.

5 marks

2 Work out the surface area and volume of these cylinders.

a) radius = 4cm

9cm

Surface area = _____ cm²

Volume = _____ cm³

b) diameter = 10cm

4.5cm

Surface area = _____ cm²

Volume = _____ cm³

8 marks

3   The diagram shows a circle inside a square of side length 4cm.

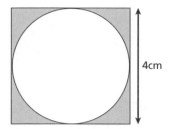

4cm

Find the total area of the shaded regions. Give your answer to 2 decimal places.

_____ cm²

3 marks

4   Barry is planning on buying a car. He visits two garages which have the following payment options:

Mike's Motors	Carol's Cars
£500 deposit	£600 deposit
36 monthly payments of £150	12 monthly payments of £50
£150 administration fee	24 monthly payments of £200

Which garage should Barry buy his car from in order to get the cheapest deal? Show your working to justify your answer.

3 marks

TOTAL

19

5 The nth term of a sequence is given by the expression $\dfrac{(n+3)(n+4)}{2}$

    a) Write down an expression in terms of n for the $(n+1)$th term.

    b) Use your two expressions to prove that the sum of two consecutive terms in the sequence is a square number.

4 marks

6 A wire 15m long runs from the top of a pole to the ground as shown in the diagram. The wire makes an angle of 45° with the ground.

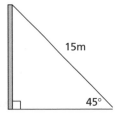

15m

45°

Calculate the height of the pole. Give your answer to a suitable degree of accuracy.

2 marks

7 Donny the magician claims to be able to read minds.

His friend Lewis asks him to prove his claim.

Donny tells Lewis to think of a number and to follow the instructions given below. Donny will know the answer.

The instructions are as follows:

Think of a number, multiply it by 2, add 10, divide by 2, and subtract the number you first thought of.

Donny tells Lewis he got the answer 5 and he is right.

Complete the table below to show why Donny's trick worked.

Instruction	Mathematical expression
Think of a number	n
Multiply by 2	
Add 10	
Divide by 2	
Subtract the number you thought of	

2 marks

8 The equation $x^3 + x = 5$ has a solution between 1 and 2.

Use trial and improvement to find the solution to 1 decimal place.

2 marks

TOTAL

10

9 A recipe for 12 cupcakes needs 80g of butter and 200g of flour.

How much butter and flour are needed to make:

a) 24 cupcakes?

....g of butter

....g of flour

b) 30 cupcakes?

....g of butter

....g of flour   4 marks

10 The mean of 7 numbers is 11.

I add another number and the mean is now 12.

What number did I add?

2 marks

11 The data gives the waiting time in minutes of 15 patients in a surgery:

49	23	34	10	28	28	25	45
39	35	15	14	48	10	20	

a) Draw a stem-and-leaf diagram to show this information.

b) Use your diagram to find the median waiting time.

3 marks

12 Thirty children were asked if they liked cycling or swimming.

Set A is those who like cycling.

Set B is those who like swimming.

a) Complete the Venn diagram.

b) How many children do not like either cycling or swimming?

c) Find P(A ∩ B)

3 marks

TOTAL

12

Answers

Pages 6–13 Revise Questions

Page 7 Quick Test

1. 35
2. 226 635
3. 163
4. 64

Page 9 Quick Test

1. 49
2. 8
3. $2 \times 2 \times 2 \times 5$
4. 252
5. 8

Page 11 Quick Test

1. $\div 2$ OR $\times \frac{1}{2}$
2. B
3. −3
4. A

Page 13 Quick Test

1. 8, 13, 18, 23, 28
2. 4, 19, 44, 79, 124
3. a) $24 - 4n$ b) −176
4. Position to term rule

Pages 14–15 Review Questions

Page 14

1. 1996 [1] because 2000 − 1996 = 4 but 2007 − 2000 = 7 [1]
2.
4	7	6	245
− 2	3	1	OR Method mark for valid
2	4	5	attempt to subtract [1]

[2]

3. 5000, 46 000, 458 000, 46 000 All 4 correct [2] Any 3 correct. [1]
4. $\frac{27}{50}$, 55%, 0.56, 0.6, 0.63
   All 5 correct [3] OR 3 out of 5 correct [2] OR 55% = 0.55 and $\frac{27}{50}$ = 0.54 [1]
5. Amy = 2×22 = 44 years old [2] OR Rashmi = 25 − 3 = 22 years old seen [1]
6. 15 878 [3]
   OR 12 000 + 1800 + 210 + 1600 + 240 + 28 [2]
   OR Valid attempt at multiplication with one numerical error [1]
7. 52 [2]
   OR Valid attempt at division with one numerical error [1]
8.

```
|_|_|_|_|_|_|_|_|_|_|_|_|_|_|_|
1       2       3       4
    ↑               ↑
```

Both correct [2] One correct [1]

Page 15

1. 200ml [3]
   OR 1000ml and 800ml seen [2]
   OR 1000ml seen [1]
2. a) 16 or 36 [1]
   b) 13 or 17 or 31 or 37 or 53 or 61 or 71 or 73 [1]
   c) 36 [1]
   d) 15 [1]
3. 9cm [2] OR 27 ÷ 3 seen [1] (an equilateral triangle has three equal sides)
4. 33 [2]
   OR 11 seen [1]

5. 25 [3]
   OR 65 seen [2]
   OR 130 seen [1]
   (angles in a triangle add up to 180°, base angles in an isosceles triangle are equal, right angle is 90°)
6. $T = 200$ [1] ($S = T + 100$, $2T + 100 = 500$) $S = 300$ [1]

Pages 16–17 Practice Questions

Page 16

1. Jessa is right as using BIDMAS multiply is first [2] OR Using BIDMAS the multiply is first [1]
2. a) £4248 [3]
   OR 3000 + 500 + 40 + 600 +100 + 8 [2]
   OR Valid attempt at multiplication with one numerical error [1]
   b) 354 ÷ 52 = 6.8 [2]
   OR Valid attempt at division with one numerical error [1]
   7 coaches needed [1]
   c) 10 spare seats [2] OR 364 seen ($52 \times 7 = 364$) [1]
3. Harry's because $3 \times 6 = £18$ but $5 \times 4 = £20$ [3]
   OR £18 and £20 seen but no conclusion [2]
   OR 15 ÷ 3 and 15 ÷ 5 seen [1]
4. −3 [1]

1. $p = 3$ [1], $q = 3$ [1], $r = 5$ [1] OR valid attempt at prime factorisation seen [1]
2. xy [2]

Page 17

1. a) $3n + 1$ [3] OR $3n$ [2] OR +3 seen as term to term rule [1]
   b) 181 [1]
2. 5, 9, 13, 17, 21 = arithmetic. 2, 8, 18, 32, 50 = quadratic. 8, 17, 32, 53, 80 = quadratic. All three correct [2] OR 1 correct [1]
3. a) $8^2 = 64$ and $9^2 = 81$ so $\sqrt{79}$ is between 8 and 9 OR attempt to find any two square numbers each side of 79 [2]
   b) 8.89 [1]

1. 2, 7, 12, 17, 22 = $5n - 3$. 3, 9, 27, 81 = 3^n. 6, 21, 46, 81, 126 = $5n^2 + 1$. 4, 3, 2, 1, 0 = $5 - n$. All 4 correct [2] 2 correct [1]
2. 25 units [2] OR attempt to divide by 2 once or more [1]

Pages 18–25 Revise Questions

Page 19 Quick Test

1. 24cm
2. 27cm²
3. 6cm²
4. 24cm, 19cm²

Page 21 Quick Test

1. 16cm²
2. 13cm²
3. Circumference = 18.8cm (1 d.p.) Area = 28.3cm² (1 d.p.)
4. Area = 5.6cm² (1 d.p.)

Page 23 Quick Test

1. a) Red = 9 Blue = 7 Green = 8 Yellow = 6 Other = 7 b) 37
2. a) 6 and 3 b) mean = 9.2 (1 d.p.) median = 6 range = 37
   c) Median as there is an outlier

Page 25 Quick Test

1. a)

	Football	Rugby	Total
Women	16	9	25
Men	20	10	30
Total	36	19	55

b) 36 c) 9 d) 55

Page 26

1. 1248 **[1]** (24 is half of 48) 26 **[1]** (26 is half of 52) 48 **[1]**
2. 15 and 12 **[2] OR** either 15 or 12 seen **[1]**
3. 4 packs of sausages and 3 packs of rolls **[3] OR** 24 seen **[2]**
   OR Valid attempt to find LCM of 6 and 8 seen **[1]**

1. a) $x = 2$ **[1]** $y = 3$ **[1]**
   b) $z = 5$ (remember $x^m \times x^n = x^{m+n}$) **[1]**
2. Can be written as $(5x)^2$ **[1]**
3. −1 and −4 **[1]**
4. No – any counter example e.g. $1 + -8 = -7$ **[2]**

Page 27

1. a) 44 **[1]** (for 20th term $n = 20$)   b) 204 **[1]**
2. $2n - 1$ **[2] OR** $2n$ seen **[1]**
3. a) 14 **[1]**   b) 9 weeks **[1]** c) $3n + 5$ **[1]**

1. Cindy is right **[1]** BIDMAS states indices first so $4 \times 100 + 2 = 402$ **[1]**
2. 28 days **[2] OR** 540/20 seen **[1]**

Page 28

1. $X = 8$cm **[1]** $Y = 6.8$cm **[1]** (area of a rectangle = L × W)
2. a) 192 **[3] OR** 16×12 seen **[2] OR** 120 000 and 625 seen **[1]**
   (As each tile is 25cm, 16 will fit along one side and 12 along the other)
   b) £300 **[2] OR** 20 seen **[1]** (The nearest multiple of 10 bigger 192 is 200)
   c) 8 tiles **[1]**

1. 20cm² **[3] OR** 10 seen as an attempt to find area of triangle **[2] OR** 2 and 5 seen as an attempt to find midpoints. **[1]**

Page 29

1. a) Phil 66.4 (1 d.p.) **[1]** Dave 68.9 (1 d.p.) **OR** attempt to add them up and divide by number of values **[1]**
   b) Phil 70 **[1]** Dave 175 **[1]**
   c) Dave as higher average **OR** Phil as more consistent **[2]**

1. 16.7mm **[3] OR** 870 seen **[2] OR** 5, 15, 30, 50 seen as midpoints **[1]**

Page 31 Quick Test

1. 100 000
2. 16.2, 16.309, 16.34, 16.705, 16.713
3. 49.491
4. 17.211
5. 335.42

Page 33 Quick Test

1. 163
2. 150 000
3. 5.69×10^5
4. 8.7×10^{-4}
5. 65 600

Page 35 Quick Test

1. $7x + 5y + 6$
2. c^2d^2
3. 26

Page 37 Quick Test

1. $8x - 4$
2. $2x - 14y$
3. $5(x - 5)$
4. $2x^3(x^2 - 2)$

Page 38

1. (This is a compound area; separate into a rectangle and triangle)
   a) 25m² **[3] OR** 20 and 5 seen **[2] OR** only 20 seen **[1]**
   b) 4 tins **[1]**
   c) £48 **[2] OR** answer to b) × 12 seen **[1]**
2. 5093 **[2] OR** 157 or 1.57 seen **[1]** (this question is about the circumference of a circle; notice the units are different, 50cm = 0.5m)

1. a) Sector B as 8.73 is bigger than 5.65 **[3] OR** 5.65 or 8.73 seen as an attempt to find area of sector **[2] OR** 28.3 or 78.5 seen as attempt to find the area of circle **[1]**
   b) Sector B, as 13.49 is bigger than 9.77 **[3] OR** 3.77 or 3.49 seen as an attempt to find an arc length **[2] OR** 18.8 or 31.4 seen as an attempt to find the circumference of a circle **[1]**

Page 39

1. 30 **[3] OR** Two-way table seen with no more than two mistakes **[2] OR** Two-way table with no more than three mistakes.

	Home	Hospital	Water	Total
Teen	2	10	4	16
Non teen	18	20	6	44
Total	20	30	10	60

2. Median as data contains an outlier (14 808 much bigger than the rest of the data and there is no mode) **[1]**

1. (To find the total multiply the mean by the number of pupils) 6.2 **[3] OR** 174 seen **[2] OR** 210 seen **[1]**
2. Mode, as this is the most common size required **[2] OR** Mode **[1]**

Page 40

1. a) 57.832 **[1]**
   b) 21.98 **[1]**
   c) 74.154 **[1]**
   d) 216 **[1]**

1. $0.02 \to 200$, $50 \to 0.08$, $8 \to 0.5$, $20 \to 0.2$
   All 4 correct **[2] OR** 2 correct **[1]**
2. a) 6.89×10^6 **[1]**   b) 8.766×10^{-3} **[1]**
   c) 59 890 000 is bigger as $5.989 \times 10^4 = 59 890$ **[1]**

Page 41

1. Both of them **[1]** $2(x + y)$ expands to $2x + 2y$ or vice versa **[1]**
2. £123 **[3] OR** 48 seen **[2] OR** 120×0.4 seen **[1]**
3. $3x + 7$ **[2] OR** $8x + 2 - 5x + 5$ seen **[1]**
4. $3a(bc + 2)$ **[2] OR** $3(abc + 2a)$ or $a(3bc + 6)$ seen **[1]** (completely means remove all factors)
5. 144 **[2] OR** 9 seen **[1]** ($ab = a \times b$)
6. $3a - b$, $2a - b$, b. All three correct **[2]** any one correct **[1]**

1. $x^2 + 2x - 8$ **[2] OR** $x^2 + 4x - 2x - 8$ **[1]** (Always remember to simplify)
2. $(x + 2)$ **[1]** $(x - 1)$ **[1]** (factorising is the opposite of expanding)
3. $(x + y)^2 = (x + y)(x + y) = x^2 + 2xy + y^2$ **[2] OR** $(x + y)^2 = (x + y)(x + y)$ **[1]**

Answers

Pages 42–49 Revise Questions

Page 43 Quick Test

1. Volume = 140cm³
   Surface area = 166cm²
2. Volume = 440cm³
   Surface area = 358cm²

Page 45 Quick Test

1. a) Volume = 603cm³
   Surface area = 402cm²
   b) Volume = 180cm³
   Surface area = 207cm²
2. 116cm³

Page 47 Quick Test

1. 20°
2. Sunday
3. No Helen still uses more (approx. mean 51).

Page 49 Quick Test

1. Own goal
2. Positive
3. The spinner is biased **OR** there is no yellow on the spinner.

Pages 50–51 Review Questions

Page 50

1. 6.765, 6.776, 7.675, 7.756, 7.765
   All five correct **[2] OR** three correct **[1]**
2. a) £15.99 **[2] OR** attempt to add three costs with only one numerical mistake **[1]**
   b) £4.01 **[1]**

1. a) £8.20 **[1]** b) £8.30 **[1]** c) 1.2% **[2] OR** $10 \div 830$ or $\frac{0.1}{8.3}$ seen **[1]**

Page 51

1. a) ab **[1]** b) $2a + 2b$ or $2(a + b)$ **[1]** c) $3a$ and $5a$ **[1]**
2. 2 **[1]** −2 **[1]**
3. $4t(2ut - u + 5)$ **[2] OR** $4(2ut^2 - ut + 5t)$ **[1] OR** $t(8ut - 4u + 20)$ **[1]**
4. Yes as $4n$ can be written as $2(2n)$ **[1]** (integer means whole number)

1. a) $x^2 - y^2$ **[1]**
   b) 800 seen with 201 and 199 substituted into the brackets **[2]**
   OR 400 and 2 seen **[1]**
2. Yes **[1]** with 190 to nearest cm, largest value 190.5. 200cm to nearest 10cm, smallest 195cm. **[1]** 195 is bigger than 190.5. **[1]**
   OR Yes **[1]** with 190.5 or 195 seen **[1] OR** Just 190.5 or 195 seen. **[1]**

Pages 52–53 Practice Questions

Page 52

1. Surface area = 117cm² **[1]**
   Volume = 81cm³ **[1]**
2. $942 \div 5^2 \div \pi$ **[1]** = 12.0cm **[1]**
3. $1385 \div 7^2 \div \pi$ **[1]** = 9.00cm **[1]**

1. Surface area = 672cm² **[1]**
   Volume = 960cm³ **[1]**
2. a) $2 \times 2 \times 10 = 40$ **[1]** $14 - 2 = 12$ **[1]** $12 \times 2 \times 2 = 48$
   $40 + 48 = 88$cm³ **[1]**
   b) $14 \times 7 \times 4 = 392$ **[1]** $5 \times 2 \times 4 = 40$ **[1]** $392 - 40 = 352$cm³ **[1]**

Page 53

1. Example answers: Speed of runner against distance, Cost of taxi against number of people in taxi, etc. **[2]**
2. Question should have a time frame (e.g.How many more times do you go shopping during the Christmas period than other times of the year?). **[2]**
   Response boxes should cover all outcomes and not overlap (e.g. about the same; 1–5 times more; 6–10 times more; more than 10 times more). **[2]**
3. Scatter, frequency polygon, pie chart, bar chart, line graph, histogram, etc. Four examples **[2]**
   Choose a graph with a reason, for instance pie chart as it shows the percentage of time spent. **[2]**
4. The girls (Helen and Rhian) use their phones more than the boys (Ian and Andy); Helen (Sunday) has the most time spent on a day closely followed by Rhian (Sunday). The weekend shows phone use to be higher. Two comparisons **[2]**

1. Hypothesis – The dice is biased **OR** has no number 8 **[1]**. Test roll the dice recording outcomes a large number of times **[1]**. If the outcomes are fairly split then the dice is not biased **[1]**.

Pages 54–61 Revise Questions

Page 55 Quick Test

1. e.g. $\frac{4}{6}, \frac{6}{9}, \frac{8}{12} \cdots$
2. $\frac{64}{77}$
3. $\frac{29}{72}$
4. $\frac{15}{52}$
5. $\frac{81}{100}$

Page 57 Quick Test

1. $\frac{1}{3}$
2. $\frac{49}{36} = 1\frac{13}{36}$
3. $\frac{28}{5} = 5\frac{3}{5}$
4. $\frac{395}{42} = 9\frac{17}{42}$

Page 59 Quick Test

1.

x	−2	−1	0	1	2	3
y	−10	−7	−4	−1	2	5

2. $y = 5x + 3$

Page 61 Quick Test

1. a) Gradient = 3, Intercept = 5
   b) Gradient = 6, Intercept = −7
   c) Gradient = −3, Intercept = 2
2.

x	−3	−2	−1	0	1	2	3
y	4	2	2	4	8	14	22

Pages 62–63 Review Questions

Page 62

1. Surface area = $2(14 \times 2) + 2(6 \times 2) + 2(14 \times 6)$ **[1]** = 248cm² **[1]**
   Volume = $14 \times 2 \times 6$ **[1]** = 168cm³ **[1]**
2. Radius = $\frac{11}{2} = 5.5$m **[1]** $5.5^2 \times \pi = 95.03$ **[1]**
   $95.03 \times 2.2 = 209$m³ **[1]**
3. $\sqrt[3]{512}$ **[1]** = 800cm **[1]**
4. No Phil does not have enough. **[1]**
   Surface area = $2(15 \times 10 + 15 \times 20 + 10 \times 20)$ **[1]** = 1300cm² **[1]**

1. Volume = $(7 \times 12 \times 6) + (3 \times 7 \times 12 \times \frac{1}{2})$ **[1]** = 504 + 126 = 630m³ **[1]**
   Surface area = $2(7 \times 6) + 2(12 \times 6) + (12 \times 7) + 2(12 \times 4) +$
   $2(3 \times 7 \times \frac{1}{2})$ **[1]** = 84 + 144 + 84 + 96 + 21 = 429m² **[1]**

Page 63

1.

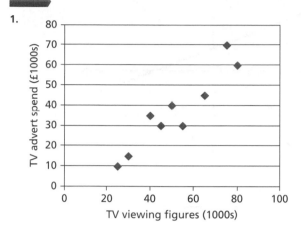

Correct axes labels **[1]**. Points plotted correctly **[1]**.
It has a positive correlation **[1]**; the more you spend on
advertising the show the more people are likely to watch. **[1]**
2. **a)** Example answers: 'a lot' is too vague – the quantity should
   be specific **[1]**; how much junk food in a period of time could be
   asked **[1]**
   b) Example answers: More answer options could be given, e.g. 0
   [1]; quantity of fruit could be more specific **[1]**

1. Example answers: Laura spends most of her time in the garden
   whereas Jules spends it watching TV. Jules doesn't walk at all and
   goes to the gym more than Laura, etc.   Three comparisons **[3]**
2. Katya could hypothesise that the spinner is biased. **[1]** She
   would test by spinning it many times **[1]** and seeing what the
   experimental probability would be for each colour. **[1]**

Pages 64–65 **Practice Questions**

Page 64

1. **a)** $\frac{21}{20} = 1\frac{1}{20}$ **[1]**
   b) $\frac{41}{40} = 1\frac{1}{40}$ **[1]**
   c) $\frac{29}{20} = 1\frac{9}{20}$ **[1]**
   d) $\frac{5}{8}$ **[1]**
   e) $\frac{3}{10}$ **[1]**
   f) $\frac{19}{36}$ **[1]**
2. **a)** $\frac{2}{24} = \frac{1}{12}$ **[1]**
   b) $\frac{40}{54} = \frac{20}{27}$ **[1]**
   c) $\frac{3}{20}$ **[1]**
3. **a)** $\frac{3}{16}$ **[1]**
   b) $\frac{9}{48}$ **[1]** = $\frac{3}{16}$ **[1]**
   c) $\frac{21}{12} + \frac{1}{2} = \frac{9}{4}$ **[1]** = $2\frac{1}{4}$ **[1]**

1. **a)** $\frac{35}{8} + \frac{11}{5} = \frac{263}{40}$ **[1]** = $6\frac{23}{40}$ **[1]**
   b) $\frac{18}{5} + \frac{21}{9} + \frac{7}{2} = \frac{283}{30}$ **[1]** = $9\frac{13}{30}$ **[1]**
   c) $\frac{29}{4} - \frac{30}{11} = \frac{199}{44}$ **[1]** = $4\frac{23}{44}$ **[1]**
   d) $\frac{11}{5} - \frac{10}{7}$ **[1]** = $\frac{27}{35}$ **[1]**

Page 65

1. (–1, 4) **[1]** and (–3, 2) **[1]**
2.

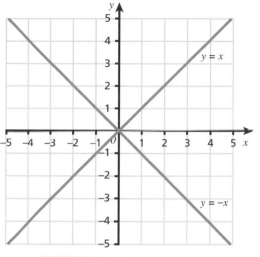

[2]

3.

x	−1	0	1	2	3
y	7	4	1	−2	−5

[2]

[2]

1. Gradient = −3 **[1]** and intercept = +4 **[1]**
2.

x	−3	−2	−1	0	1	2	3
y	16	8	2	−2	−4	−4	−2

All correct **[3]**; At least five correct **[2]**; At least three correct **[1]**

Pages 66–73 **Revise Questions**

Page 67 Quick Test
1. Student's own drawings
2. **a)** 76° **b)** 56° **c)** 65°

Page 69 Quick Test
1. **a)** 55° **b)** 112° **c)** 126°
2. Two of equilateral triangle, square or hexagon

Page 71 Quick Test
1. Likely
2. Student's own drawing
3. **a)** $\frac{1}{3}$ **b)** $\frac{2}{3}$
4. 0.228

Page 73 Quick Test
1. **a)** 0.47 **b)** 0.53 **c)** 9.5 so 9 or 10

Page 74

1. a) $\frac{4}{10} + \frac{1}{10} = \frac{5}{10} = \frac{1}{2}$ [1]

   b) $\frac{7}{12} + \frac{3}{12} = \frac{10}{12} = \frac{5}{6}$ [1]

   c) $\frac{5}{30} + \frac{6}{30} = \frac{11}{30}$ [1]

   d) $\frac{20}{70} + \frac{21}{70} = \frac{41}{70}$ [1]

   e) $\frac{8}{9} - \frac{3}{9} = \frac{5}{9}$ [1]

   f) $\frac{14}{22} - \frac{11}{22}$ [1] $= \frac{3}{22}$ [1]

   g) $\frac{27}{30} - \frac{20}{30}$ [1] $= \frac{7}{30}$ [1]

2. a) $\frac{4}{45}$ [1]

   b) $\frac{9}{70}$ [1]

   c) $\frac{10}{36} = \frac{5}{18}$ [1]

   d) $\frac{2}{9} \times \frac{4}{1}$ [1] $= \frac{8}{9}$ [1]

   e) $\frac{4}{5} \times \frac{11}{6} = \frac{44}{30}$ [1] $= \frac{22}{15} = 1\frac{7}{15}$ [1]

3. $\frac{2}{5} + \frac{1}{4} = \frac{8}{20} + \frac{5}{20}$ [1] $= \frac{13}{20}$
   $1 - \frac{13}{20}$ [1] $= \frac{7}{20}$ [1]

4. $\frac{4}{9} + \frac{1}{3} = \frac{7}{9}$ [1] $1 - \frac{7}{9} = \frac{2}{9}$ [1]
   Shared equally $= \frac{1}{9}$ chocolate [1]

1. a) $\frac{77}{9}$ [1]

   b) $\frac{23}{7}$ [1]

   c) $\frac{14}{11}$ [1]

Page 75

1.

x	−1	0	1	2	3
y	−6	−4	−2	0	2

[2]

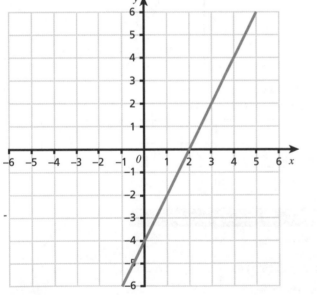

[2]

2.

x	−3	−2	−1	0	1	2	3
y	−5	−5	−3	1	7	15	25

All correct [3]; At least five correct [2]; At least three correct [1].

1. $y = x^2 - 4x + 6$
   $x = 3$: $3^2 - 4(3) + 6 = y = 3$. So, yes [1] (3, 3) is a coordinate on the graph as when $x = 3$, $y = 3^2 - 4(3) + 6 = 3$ [1]

2. $x = \frac{1}{2}$ [1]
   $y = 4$ [1]

$y = 4x + 2$ $y = -2x + 5$ [1]

3. a) and e) [1]
   b) and d) [1]
   c) and f) [1]

Page 76

1. $180 - 106 = 74$ [1], $74 \times 2 = 148$, $180 - 148 = 32°$ [1]

2. a) $x = 134°$ [1] as alternate (Z angle), $y = 180 - 134 = 46°$ [1]
   b) $x = 180 - 53 = 127°$ [1], $y = 127°$ [1] as it is a corresponding angle (F angle)

3. Decagon [1]

4. $180 - 150 = 30°$ (exterior angle) [1]
   $\frac{360}{30} = 12$ sides [1]

1. One possibility:

[3]

Page 77

1. $1 - 0.65$ [1] $= 0.35$ [1] (Probability of all outcomes take away probability of landing other way up.)

2. a)

Number	Frequency	Estimated probability
1	5	$\frac{5}{50} = \frac{1}{10}$
2	8	$\frac{8}{50} = \frac{4}{25}$
3	7	$\frac{7}{50}$
4	7	$\frac{7}{50}$
5	8	$\frac{8}{50} = \frac{4}{25}$
6	15	$\frac{15}{50} = \frac{3}{10}$
Total 50		1

All correct [3]; At least five rows correct [2]; At least three rows correct [1].

   b) i) $\frac{3}{10}$ [1]

      ii) $\frac{5}{50} + \frac{7}{50} + \frac{8}{50} = \frac{20}{50} = \frac{2}{5}$ [1]

      iii) $\frac{15}{50} + \frac{8}{50} = \frac{23}{50}$ [1]

   c) The dice is unlikely to be fair [1] as the probability of getting a 6 is a lot higher than the theoretical $\frac{1}{6}$ [1].

1. a)

Yellow	Red	Blue	Green	Pink
0.26	0.18	0.09	0.32	0.15

[1]

b) $1 - 0.26$ **[1]** $= 0.74$ **[1]**

c) $0.09 + 0.32 = 0.41$ [1]

Pages 78–85 Revise Questions

Page 79 Quick Test

1. 0.35, 35%
2. £28
3. £49

Page 81 Quick Test

1. £405
2. £92 000
3. 84%
4. 80%
5. £460
6. £150 000

Page 83 Quick Test

1. 5
2. $y = 5$
3. $x = -9$
4. $x = 4$
5. $x = 2$

Page 85 Quick Test

1. 11
2. 3kg
3. 1.8
4. 2.2
5. 5.6

Pages 86–87 Review Questions

Page 86

1. a) $x = 180 - 61 = 119°$ [2]

$y = 119°$ (as it is corresponding)

b) $y = 180 - 114 = 66°$

$x = 66°$ (as it is alternate angle) [2]

2. 1260° [1]

3. $180 - 160 = 20°$ **[1]**

$\frac{360}{20}$ **[1]** = 18, so it is an 18–sided shape. **[1]**

1. A regular pentagon has an interior angle of 108° **[1]**. 108 is not a factor of 360 **[1]** so therefore the tessellation would either create an overlap or a gap. **[1]**

2.

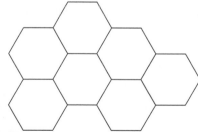

[2]

Page 87

1. a)

Sprinkles	Frequency	Probability
Chocolate	19	$\frac{19}{50} = 0.38$
Hundreds and thousands	14	$\frac{14}{50} = 0.28$
Strawberry	7	$\frac{7}{50} = 0.14$
Nuts	10	$\frac{10}{50} = 0.2$

All correct **[2]**; At least two rows correct **[1]**.

b) $\frac{19}{50} + \frac{10}{50}$ **[1]** $= \frac{29}{50}$ or 0.58 **[1]**

2. $1 - 0.47 = 0.53$ [1]

3. a)

Sales destination	Probability of going to destination
London	0.26
Cardiff	0.15
Chester	0.2
Manchester	0.39

[1]

b) Cardiff (it has the lowest probability) [1]

1. 0.68×325 **[1]** $= 221$ claims **[1]**

2. $1 - 0.14 = 0.86$ **[1]**

$0.86 \times 250 = 215$ bread rolls that are good **[1]**

Pages 88–89 Practice Questions

Page 88

1.

Fraction	Decimal	Percentage	
$\frac{3}{5}$	0.6	60	[1]
$\frac{55}{100} = \frac{11}{20}$	0.55	55	[1]
$\frac{32}{100} = \frac{8}{25}$	0.32	32	[1]
$\frac{3}{100}$	0.03	3	[1]

2. a) $15 \div 3 \times 2$ [1]

$= \$10$ [1]

b) $210 \div 7 \times 3$ [1]

$= \$90$ [1]

c) $27 \div 9 \times 4$ [1]

$= \$12$ [1]

1. a) 10% of 80cm = $80 \div 10 = 8$cm

$5\% = 8 \div 2 = 4$cm [1]

$15\% = 8 + 4 = 12$cm [1]

b) 10% of 160m = $160 \div 10 = 16$m

$30\% = 16 \times 3 = 48$m [1]

$5\% = 16 \div 2 = 8$m [1]

$35\% = 48 + 8 = 56$m [1]

c) $10\% = 70 \div 10 = \$7$ [1]

$5\% = 7 \div 2 = \$3.50$ [1]

2. 10% of £75 = $75 \div 10 = £7.50$

$20\% = £7.50 \times 2 = £15$ [1]

Sale price = £75 − £15 [1]

$= £60$ [1]

3. a) $300 \div 10 = 30$

$5\% = £15$ [1]

After two years $£15 \times 2 = £30$ [1]

Total in account = £330 [1]

b) $300 \div 10 = 30$

$5\% = £15$ [1]

After five years $£15 \times 5 = £75$ [1]

Total in account = £375 [1]

Page 89

1. a) $2x - 5 = 3$

$(+5)\ 2x = 8$ [1]

$(\div 2)\ \ x = 4$ [1]

b) $\ \ \ \ 3x + 1 = x + 7$

$(-x)\ 2x + 1 = 7$ [1]

$(-1)\ 2x = 6$

$(\div 2)\ \ \ x = 3$ [1]

c) $2(2x - 3) = x - 3$
$\quad\quad 4x - 6 = x - 3$
$(-x)\quad 3x - 6 = -3$ [1]
$(+6)\quad 3x = 3$
$(\div 3)\quad x = 1$ [1]

d) $\frac{3x+5}{4} = 5$
$(\times 4)\quad 3x + 5 = 20$ [1]
$(-5)\quad 3x = 15$
$(\div 3)\quad x = 5$ [1]

2. $3n + 2 = 11$ [1]
$(-2)\quad 3n = 9$
$(\div 3)\quad n = 3$ [1]

3. $4n = 48$ [1]
$\quad n = 48 \div 4$
$\quad n = 12$, so 12 people at party [1]

1. $\quad\quad 3(x + 1) = 2 + 4(2 - x)$
$\quad\quad 3x + 3 = 2 + 8 - 4x$
$\quad\quad 3x + 3 = 10 - 4x$ [1]
$(+4x)\quad 7x + 3 = 10$ [1]
$(-3)\quad 7x = 7$
$(\div 7)\quad x = 1$ [1]

2. $\quad 5(2a + 1) + 3(3a - 4) = 4(3a - 6)$
$\quad\quad 10a + 5 + 9a - 12 = 12a - 24$
$\quad\quad 19a - 7 = 12a - 24$ [1]
$(-12a)\quad 7a - 7 = -24$ [1]
$(+7)\quad 7a = -17$
$(\div 7)\quad a = -2\frac{3}{7}$ [1]

3. $x^3 - x = 50$ try $x = 3$: $3^3 - 3 = 24$ too small
   try $x = 4$: $4^3 - 4 = 60$ too big [1]
   try $x = 3.5$: $3.5^3 - 3.5 = 39.375$ too small [1]
   try $x = 3.8$: $3.8^3 - 3.8 = 51.072$ too big
   try $x = 3.7$: $3.7^3 - 3.7 = 46.953$ too small
   try $x = 3.75$ $3.75^3 - 3.75 = 48.984375$ too small [1]
As 3.8 is too big and 3.75 is too small, $x = 3.8$ (1 d.p.) [1]

4. Try $x = 7$: $7^2 + 2 \times 7 = 49 + 14 = 63$ (too small)
   Try $x = 8$: $8^2 + 2 \times 8 = 64 + 16 = 80$ (too big) [1]
   Try $x = 7.5$: $7.5^2 + 2 \times 7.5 = 56.25 + 15 = 71.25$ (too small) [1]
   Try $x = 7.8$: $7.8^2 + 2 \times 7.8 = 60.84 + 15.6$ (too big)
   $\quad\quad\quad = 76.44$
   Try $x = 7.7$: $7.7^2 + 2 \times 7.7 = 59.29 + 15.4$ (too small)
   $\quad\quad\quad = 74.69$
   Try $x = 7.75$: $7.75^2 + 2 \times 7.75 = 60.0625 + 15.5$
   $\quad\quad\quad = 75.5625$ (too big)
   Try $x = 7.74$: $7.74^2 + 2 \times 7.74 = 59.9076 + 15.48$
   $\quad\quad\quad = 75.3876$ (too big) [1]
   $x = 7.7$ (1 d.p.) [1]

5. $4x + 10 = 6x + 6$ **[2]** for correct equation **OR [1]** for any correct perimeter.
$(-4x)\quad 10 = 2x + 6$ [1]
$(-6)\quad 4 = 2x$
$(\div 2)\quad x = 2$ [1]

Pages 90–97 Revise Questions

Page 91 Quick Test
1. 6
2. a)   b)

3. a)

   b) Rectangle 3cm × 6cm

Page 93 Quick Test
1. Any three shapes exactly the same size
2. D

3. 4m
4. A and B
5. Any two similar shapes

Page 95 Quick Test
1. a) 6 : 8 b) 8 : 6
2. a) 1 : 3 b) 7 : 1 c) 1 : 4

Page 97 Quick Test
1. 10 : 25 : 5
2. Sara £200, John £160
3. 28
4. £36
5. 4 days

Pages 98–99 Review Questions

Page 98

1. a) $\frac{13}{25} = \frac{52}{100} = 52\%$ [1]
   b) $0.375 = \frac{375}{1000}$ **[1]** $= \frac{3}{8}$ **[1]**
   c) $36\% = \frac{36}{100}$ [1]
   $\quad\quad = \frac{9}{25}$ [1]
2. a) $5 \div 5 \times 2$ [1]
   $\quad\quad = £2$ [1]
   b) $£5 - (£2.50 + £2)$ [1]
   $\quad\quad = £0.50$ or 50p [1]
3. a) 10% of 300cm $= 300 \div 10 = 30$cm
   $\quad 20\% = 30 \times 2$ [1]
   $\quad\quad = 60$cm [1]
   b) 10% of $140 = 140 \div 10 = $14
   $\quad 5\% = 14 \div 2 = $7 [1]
   $\quad 1\% = 140 \div 100 = $1.40 [1]
   $\quad 6\% = $7 + $1.40 = $8.40 [1]
   c) 10% of 2800 $= 2800 \div 10 = 280$g
   $\quad 30\% = 280 \times 3 = 840$g [1]
   $\quad 5\% = 280 \div 2 = 140$g [1]
   $\quad 35\% = 840 + 140 = 980$g [1]
4. 10% of £90 $= 90 \div 10 = $£9
   $\quad 5\% = £9 \div 2 = £4.50$ [1]
   $\quad 15\% = £9 + £4.50 = £13.50$ [1]
   Sale price $= £90 - £13.50$
   $\quad\quad = £76.50$ [1]
5. a) $150 \div 100 \times 6$
   $\quad 6\% = £9$ [1]
   Total in account after one year $= £159$ [1]
   b) $150 \div 100 \times 6$
   $\quad 6\% = £9$ [1]
   After four years $£9 \times 4 = £36$ [1]
   Total in account $= £186$ [1]

1. $\frac{3}{25}$ $\frac{7}{50}$ 16%   0.18   0.2
All correct **[2]**; Three in correct order **[1]**

Page 99

1. a) $\quad\quad 6x - 5 = 4x + 7$
   $(-4x)\quad 2x - 5 = 7$
   $(+5)\quad 2x = 12$ [1]
   $(\div 2)\quad x = 6$ [1]
   b) $\quad\quad 5(x + 2) = 2(x - 1)$
   $\quad\quad 5x + 10 = 2x - 2$ [1]
   $(-2x)\quad 3x + 10 = -2$ [1]
   $(-10)\quad 3x = -12$
   $(\div 3)\quad x = -4$ [1]
   c) $\quad\quad 3x - 1 = 4 - 2x$
   $(+2x)\quad 5x - 1 = 4$ [1]
   $(+1)\quad 5x = 5$ [1]
   $(\div 5)\quad x = 1$ [1]
   d) $\quad\quad \frac{6x-5}{4} = 7$
   $(\times 4)\quad 6x - 5 = 28$ [1]
   $(+5)\quad 6x = 33$
   $(\div 6)\quad x = 5.5$ [1]

2. $56 - n = 29$ **[1]**
$\quad\quad n = 56 - 29 = 27$
$\quad$ 27 chocolate bars were sold. **[1]**
3. $\frac{20n + 150}{4} = 50$ **[1]**
$\quad$ ($\times 4$) $\;20n + 150 = 200$ **[1]**
$\quad$ (-150) $\quad\;\; 20n = 50$
$\quad$ ($\div 20$) $\quad\quad\;\; n = 2.5$
$\quad$ The builders worked for $2\frac{1}{2}$ hours. **[1]**

1. $4(x - 2) - 2(3 - 2x) = 5x + 1$
$\quad\quad\;\; 4x - 8 - 6 + 4x = 5x + 1$
$\quad\quad\quad\quad\; 8x - 14 = 5x + 1$ **[1]**
$\quad$ ($-5x$) $\quad\quad 3x - 14 = 1$ **[1]**
$\quad$ ($+14$) $\quad\quad\quad 3x - 15$
$\quad$ ($\div 3$) $\quad\quad\quad\quad\; x = 5$ **[1]**
2. $8 - 2a = 6a + 12$ **[1]**
$\quad$ ($+2a$) $\quad 8 = 8a + 12$
$\quad$ (-12) $-4 = 8a$ **[1]**
$\quad$ ($\div 8$) $-0.5 = a$ **[1]**
3. $3x^2 - 2x = 70$

try $x = 5$:	$3 \times 5^2 - 10 = 65$	too small
try $x = 6$:	$3 \times 6^2 - 12 = 96$	too big
try $x = 5.5$:	$3 \times 5.5^2 - 11 = 79.75$	too big
try $x = 5.3$:	$3 \times 5.3^2 - 10.6 = 73.67$	still too big
try $x = 5.2$:	$3 \times 5.2^2 - 10.4 = 70.72$	still too big
try $x = 5.1$	$3 \times 5.1^2 - 10.2 = 67.83$	too small
try $x = 5.15$	$3 \times 5.15^2 - 10.3 = 69.2675$	too small

[1]
[1]

As 5.2 is too big and 5.15 is too small, $x = 5.2$ (to 1 d.p.) **[1]**
[1]

Pages 100–101 Practice Questions

Page 100

1.

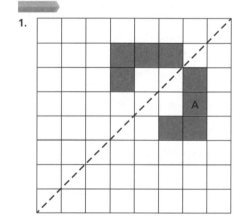

1. a) See diagram below **[2]**
$\quad$ **b)** See diagram below **[2]**

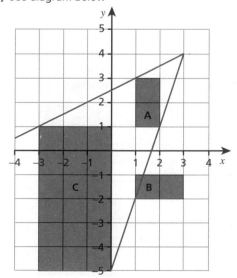

c) A and B **[1]**
d) A and C **OR** B and C **[1]**
2. $13 \div 2$ **[1]** $= 6.5$cm **[1]**

Page 101

1. $2 : 7$ **[1]**
2. a) $1 : 3$ **[1]**
$\quad$ **b)** 40 minutes : 90 minutes **[1]**
$\quad\quad$ $4 : 9$ **[1]**
$\quad$ **c)** 300 cents : 80 cents **[1]**
$\quad\quad$ $15 : 4$ **[1]**
3. $480 \div 12 = 40$ **[1]**
$\quad$ Ann: $4 \times 40 = £160$
$\quad$ Ben: $5 \times 40 = £200$
$\quad$ Cara: $3 \times 40 = £120$ **[2]**
4. 3 parts $= £27$
$\quad$ 1 part $= 27 \div 3 = £9$ **[1]**
$\quad$ 2 parts $= £9 \times 2 = £18$ **[1]**
$\quad$ Total sum of money $= £27 + £18 = £45$ **[1]**

1. Butter: $40 \div 6 \times 15 = 100$g **[1]**
$\quad$ Flour: $100 \div 6 \times 15 = 250$g **[1]**
2. a) 1 man takes $8 \times 10 = 80$ days **[1]**
$\quad\quad$ 10 men take $80 \div 10 = 8$ days **[1]**
$\quad$ **b)** 1 man takes $8 \times 10 = 80$ days **[1]**
$\quad\quad$ 5 men take $80 \div 5 = 16$ days **[1]**

Pages 102–109 Revise Questions

Page 103 Quick Test
1. a) 40km $\quad$ **b)** 16km
2. a) 19 miles $\quad$ **b)** 25 miles
3. a) £3 $\quad$ **b)** £4

Page 105 Quick Test
1. 1.5h
2. 80km/h
3. Kamala (21km/h, John 20km/h)
4. €240
5. 250g

Page 107 Quick Test
1. a) 10.24 $\quad$ **b)** 244.9225
2. a) 70 $\quad$ **b)** 6.3
3. 5.46cm
4. 7.94cm

Page 109 Quick Test
1. a) 0.3420 $\quad$ **b)** 0.8660 $\quad$ **c)** 1
2. a) 56.5° $\quad$ **b)** 55.2° $\quad$ **c)** 88.2°

Pages 110–111 Review Questions

Page 110

1.

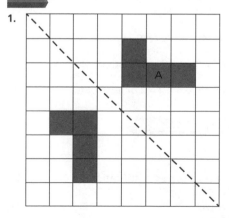

[2]

1. a) See diagram [2]
b) See diagram [2]

c) Area shape A = 1cm² [1]
d) Area shape C = 4cm² [1]
e) 1 : 4 [1]
2. 11.25 ÷ 9 = 1.25 [1]
6.4 × 1.25 = 8cm [1]

Page 111

1. a) 2 : 3 [1]
b) 25 cents : 200 cents [1]
1 : 8 [1]
c) 750m : 200m [1]
15 : 4 [1]
2. a) 40 : 15 [1]
b) 7 : 12 [1]
c) 6 : 7.5 [1]
3. 40 ÷ 8 = 5 [1]
3 parts = 5 × 3 = 15
5 parts = 5 × 5 = 25
Ratio = 15 pens : 25 pens [1]
4. 4 parts = £120
1 part = 120 ÷ 4 = £30 [1]
3 parts = £30 × 3 = £90 [1]
Altogether there is £30 + £120 + £90 = £240 [1]

1. a) In 1 hour the machine can make 1140 ÷ 8 = 142.5 cups [1]
In 10 hours the machine can make 142.5 × 10 = 1425 cups [1]
b) In 1 hour the machine can make 1140 ÷ 8 = 142.5 cups [1]
In 12 hours the machine can make 142.5 × 12 = 1710 cups [1]
2. 1 man takes 3 × 2 = 6 days [1]
3 men will take 6 ÷ 3 = 2 days [1]
3. 1 bag will feed 1 donkey for 2 days. [1]
4 bags will feed 4 donkeys for 2 days. [1]
10 bags will feed 4 donkeys for 5 days. [1]
OR
In 1 day, 3 donkeys will eat 12 ÷ 8 = 1.5 bags of oats.
In 1 day, 1 donkey will eat 1.5 ÷ 3 = 0.5 bags of oats. [1]
In 1 day, 4 donkeys will eat 0.5 × 4 = 2 bags of oats. [1]
So 10 bags will last 4 donkeys 10 ÷ 2 = 5 days. [1]

Pages 112–113 Practice Questions

Page 112

1. Indicates France and gives a correct justification [1]
Converts $ and € to £

1 000 000 ÷ 2.7 = £370 370 [1]
780 000 ÷ 1.54 = £506 494

OR
Converts $ into €
1 000 000 ÷ 2.7 × 1.54 = 570 370
OR
Converts € into $
780 000 ÷ 1.54 × 2.7 = 1 367 532
2. Speed = distance ÷ time
= 350km ÷ 1.1h [1]
= 318km/h [1]

> Be careful when using answers in further calculations.

1. a) Density = mass ÷ volume
= 2000 ÷ 0.5 [1]
= 4000kg/m³ [1]

b) Volume = mass ÷ density
= 5000kg ÷ 4000kg/m³ [1]
Volume = 1.25m³ [1]

Page 113

1. a) $2^2 + 5^2 = BC^2$
$BC = \sqrt{29}$ [1]
BC = 5.39m [1]
b) $9^2 + AC^2 = 17^2$
$AC = \sqrt{289 - 81} = \sqrt{208}$ [1]
AC = 14.4cm [1]
2. a) $\sin 25 = \frac{p}{17}$
$p = \sin 25 \times 17$ [1]
p = 7.18m [1]
b) $\tan y = \frac{32}{46}$
$y = \tan^{-1}(32 \div 46)$ [1]
y = 34.8° [1]

1. $\cos x = \frac{8}{20}$ [1]
$x = \cos^{-1}(8 \div 20)$ [1]
x = 66.4° [1]
2. a) No [1]
b) Yes [1]
c) No [1]
d) Yes [1]

Pages 114–115 Review Questions

Page 114

1. a) 200 ÷ 1.75 [1]
= £114.29 [1]
b) 200 × 1.75 [1]
= US$350 [1]
2. a) Time = 300 ÷ 40 [1]
= 7.5 hours [1]
b) Distance = 40 × 4 [1]
= 160 miles [1]

1. a)

Time (t minutes)	No. of bacteria
0	1
10	2
20	4
30	8
40	16
50	32
60	64
70	128
80	256
90	512
100	1024

[2]

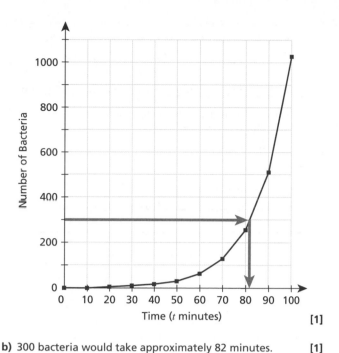

[1]

b) 300 bacteria would take approximately 82 minutes. [1]

Page 115

1. **a)** $\tan x = \frac{15}{8}$
   $x = \tan^{-1}(15 \div 8)$ [1]
   $x = 61.9°$ [1]
   b) $23^2 + 15^2 = x^2$
   $x = \sqrt{754}$ [1]
   $x = 27.5\text{m}$ [1]
2. **a)** $\sin 30° = \frac{3}{y}$
   $y = 3 \div \sin 30°$ [1]
   $y = 6\text{cm}$ [1]
   b) $6^2 + AB^2 = 9^2$
   $AB = \sqrt{81 - 36} = \sqrt{45}$ [1]
   $AB = 6.7\text{cm}$ [1]
3. $\sin 35° = \frac{\text{opp}}{18}$
   $\sin 35° \times 18 = \text{height}$ [1]
   Height of the pole = 10.3m [1]

1. **a)** $6.4^2 + h^2 = 15^2$
   $h = \sqrt{225 - 40.96} = \sqrt{184.04}$ [1]
   $h = 13.57\text{m}$ [1]
   b) $\cos x = \frac{6.4}{15}$
   $x = \cos^{-1}(6.4 \div 15)$ [1]
   $x = 64.7°$ [1]

Pages 116–127 Mixed Test-Style Questions

Pages 116–121 No Calculator Allowed
1. **a)** Surface Area = $2(6 \times 4 + 6 \times 2 + 4 \times 2) = 88\text{cm}^2$ [1]
   Volume = $6 \times 4 \times 2 = 48\text{cm}^3$ [1]
   b) Surface Area = $2(12 \times 7 + 12 \times 8 + 7 \times 8) = 472\text{cm}^2$ [1]
   Volume = $12 \times 7 \times 8 = 672\text{cm}^3$ [1]
2. **a)** $4\frac{1}{2} + 2\frac{1}{3} = \frac{9}{2} + \frac{7}{3} = 6\frac{5}{6}$ [1]
   b) $5\frac{2}{3} + 8\frac{1}{4} = \frac{17}{3} + \frac{33}{4} = 13\frac{11}{12}$ [1]
   c) $9\frac{1}{6} - 2\frac{3}{8} = \frac{55}{6} - \frac{19}{8} = 6\frac{19}{24}$ [1]
   d) $12\frac{1}{2} - 14\frac{5}{6} = \frac{25}{2} - \frac{89}{6} = -2\frac{1}{3}$ [1]

3. **a)** [1]

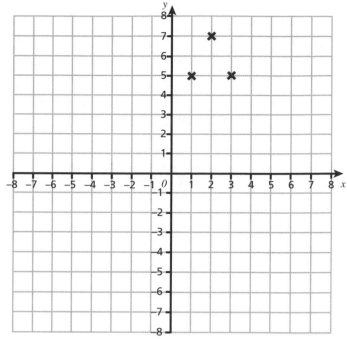

b) (2, 3) [1]

4. **a)**

x	−2	−1	0	1	2	3
y	7	5	3	1	−1	−3

All correct **[2]**; At least three correct **[1]**

b)

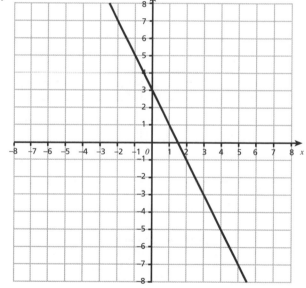

Correctly plotted line **[2]**; Straight line passing through one of the correct coordinates **[1]**

5. a) $x = 115°$ (corresponding and opposite), $y = 55°$
   (alternate) [2]
   b) $x = 180 - 75 = 105°$, $y = 180 - 85 = 95°$ [2]
6. a) i) $4x + 4y$ [1]
      ii) $3g + 1$ [1]
   b) i) $4x - 20$ [1]
      ii) $4x^2 + 16x$ [1]
   c) i) $6(x - 2)$ [1]
      ii) $4x(x - 2)$ [1]
7. $Z = 2$ [3]; 2 marks if 9 is seen; 1 mark for a correct attempt to find the area of the trapezium with no more than one numerical error.
8. a) -2 and -3 [1]
   b) 8 and -1 [1]
9. a) $4c + 4b - 4a$ or equivalent [2]; 1 mark if $b - a$ is seen.
   b) 24 [2]; 1 mark for an attempt to substitute into answer from part a).
10. a) $400 + 40 = 440$mm [1]
    b) $440 + 44 = 484$mm [1]
11. a) $y = 5$ [2]; 1 mark for $3y = 15$
    b) $x = 32$ [2]; 1 mark for $12 - x = -20$ or $\frac{x}{4} = 8$

12.

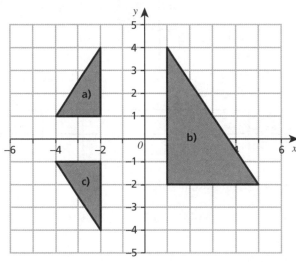

[3]

Pages 122–127 Calculator Allowed

1. a)

Type	Frequency	Probability
tug boat	12	$\frac{12}{40} = \frac{3}{10}$
ferry boat	2	$\frac{2}{40} = \frac{1}{20}$
sail boat	16	$\frac{16}{40} = \frac{2}{5}$
speed boat	10	$\frac{10}{40} = \frac{1}{4}$

[4]

   b) $\frac{2}{5} \times 75 = 30$ [1]
2. a) Surface Area = 326.7cm² [2]; 1 mark for $8 \times \pi \times 9 + 2(4^2 \times \pi)$
      Volume = 452.4 cm³ [2]; 1 mark for $4^2 \times \pi \times 9$
   b) Surface Area = 298.5cm² [2]; 1 mark for $10 \times \pi \times 4.5 + 2(5^2 \times \pi)$
      Volume = 353.4cm³ [2]; 1 mark for $5^2 \times \pi \times 4.5$
3. 3.43cm² (to 2 d.p.) [3]; 2 marks for 16 **and** $\pi(2^2)$ or 12.56637 seen; 1 mark for 16 **or** $\pi(2^2)$ or 12.56637 seen.

> Find the area of the square and subtract the area of the circle. Remember the diameter of the circle is the same as the side length of the square, in this case 4cm.

4. Carol's cars and £6000 and £6050 seen [3]; 2 marks for £6000 and £6050 seen but no conclusion; 1 mark for £5400 or other correct calculation.
5. a) $\frac{(n + 4)(n + 5)}{2}$ [1]
   b) $\frac{(n + 4)(n + 5) + (n + 3)(n + 4)}{2} = n^2 + 8n + 16 = (n + 4)^2$ [3];
      2 marks for $n^2 + 8n + 16$ seen; 1 mark for $\frac{(n + 4)(n + 5) + (n + 3)(n + 4)}{2}$ seen.
6. 10.6m [2]; 1 mark for $\sin 45 \times 15$
7.

Instruction	Mathematical expression
Think of a number	n
Multiply by 2	$2n$
Add 10	$2n + 10$
Divide by 2	$n + 5$
Subtract the number you thought of	5

All correct [2]; At least two correct [1]

8. $x = 1.5$ [2]; 1 mark for some working similar to that below:

x	x^3	$x^3 + x$	b/s
1	1	2	s
2	8	10	b
1.5	3.375	4.875	s
1.7	4.913	6.613	b
1.6	4.096	5.696	b
1.55	3.723875	5.273875	b
		$x = 1.5$ (1 d.p.)	

9. a) 160g of butter [1], 400g of flour [1]
   b) 200g of butter [1], 500g of flour [1]
10. 19 [2]; 1 mark for 96 or 77 seen.
11. a)

```
1 | 0  0  4  5
2 | 0  3  5  8  8
3 | 4  5  9
4 | 5  8  9
```

   Key: $2 | 0 = 20$ minutes
   Correct diagram with key [2]; Correct diagram only [1]
   b) 28 minutes [1]
12. a) 7 inserted in the blank part of the circle for Set A [1]
    b) 3 [1]
    c) $\frac{15}{30}$ or $\frac{1}{2}$ [1]

Glossary

a

alternate   angles which are created on a set of parallel lines are the same on a 'Z' angle.

angle   the space (usually measured in degrees) between two intersecting lines or surfaces at or close to the point where they meet.

area   the space inside a 2D shape.

arithmetic sequence   a sequence of numbers with a common difference.

axis   a line that provides scale on a graph. Often referred to as x-axis (horizontal) and y-axis (vertical).

b

biased   a statistical event where the outcomes are not equally likely.

bisect   to cut exactly in two.

bracket   symbols used to enclose a sum.

c

centre of enlargement   the position from which the enlargement of a shape will take place.

centre of rotation   the point about which a shape is rotated.

certain   an outcome of an event which must happen, probability equals 1.

chart   a visual display of data.

circle   a round 2D shape.

circumference   the perimeter of a circle.

class interval   the width of the group (difference between the upper and lower limit of the group).

composite or compound   a complex 2D or 3D shape made from several simpler shapes.

congruent   exactly the same.

constant   a value that doesn't change.

conversion   to change from one unit to another.

coordinates   usually given by x and y, the x value is the position horizontally, the y value the position vertically.

correlation   the relationship between data, the 'pattern'. Can be positive or negative.

corresponding   angles which are created on a set of parallel lines are the same on an 'F' angle.

cos   the ratio of the adjacent side to the hypotenuse in a right-angled triangle.

cylinder   a 3D shape with a circular top and base of the same size.

d

data   a collection of answers or values linked to a question or subject.

decimal places   the number of places after the decimal point.

decimal point   a point used to separate the whole part of a number from the fraction part.

decimals   numbers that contain tenths, hundredths, etc.

decrease   to make smaller.

degree   the unit of measure of an angle.

denominator   the bottom number of a fraction.

density   the mass of something per unit of volume.

diameter   the distance across a circle, going through the centre.

difference   subtraction.

direct proportion

direct proportion   quantities are in direct proportion if their ratio stays the same as the quantities increase or decrease.

distance   length.

divide   to share.

double   multiply by 2.

e

edge   a line where two faces meet in a 3D shape.

enlargement   a shape made bigger or smaller.

equation   a mathematical statement containing an equals sign.

equivalent   the same as.

estimate   a simplified calculation (not exact) often rounding to 1 s.f.

even chance   equally likely chance of an event happening or not happening.

event   a set of possible outcomes from a particular experiment.

expand   remove brackets by multiplying.

experimental probability   the ratio of the number of times an event happens to the total number of trials.

exponential   when the rate of increase gets bigger and bigger.

expression   a collection of algebraic terms.

exterior angle   an angle outside a polygon formed between one side and the adjacent side extended.

f

face   a side of a 3D shape.

factor   a number that divides exactly into another number.

factorise   take out the highest common factor and add brackets.

formula   a rule linking two or more variables.

fraction   any part of a number or 'whole'.

frequency   the number of times 'something' occurs.

function machine   flow diagram which shows the order in which operations should be carried out.

g

geometric sequence   a sequence of numbers with a common ratio.

gradient   the measure of steepness of a line.

graph   a diagram used to display information.

grouped data   data which has been sorted into groups.

h

highest common factor   the highest factor two or more numbers have in common.

hypotenuse   the longest side of a right-angled triangle.

hypothesis   a prediction of an experiment or outcome.

i

impossible   an outcome of an event which cannot happen, probability equals 0.

improper fraction   a fraction where the numerator is larger than the denominator.

increase   to make bigger.

index   the power to which a number is raised. In 2^4 the base is 2 and the index is 4.

integer   whole number.

intercept   the point at which a graph crosses the y-axis.

interest   an amount added on or taken off.

interior angle the measure of an angle inside a shape.

interpreting to describe the trends shown in a statistical diagram or statistical measure; the way in which a representation of information is used or surmised.

inverse the opposite of.

inverse proportion quantities are in inverse proportion when one decreases as the other increases.

k

key statement or code to explain a mathematical diagram.

l

likely a word used to describe a probability which is between evens and certain on a probability scale.

line of best fit the straight line (usually on a scatter graph) that represents the closest possible line to each point; shows the trend of the relationship.

linear in one direction, straight.

lowest common multiple the lowest multiple two or more numbers have in common.

lowest terms a simplified answer.

m

mean a measure of average: sum of all the values divided by the number of values.

median a measure of average: the middle value when data is ordered.

mixed number a number with a whole part and a fraction.

mode a measure of average; the most common

mutually exclusive events that have no outcomes in common.

n

negative below zero.

net a 2D representation of a 3D shape, i.e. a 3D shape has been 'unfolded'.

nth term see *position to term*.

numerator the top number of a fraction.

o

ordinary number a number not written in standard form.

outlier a statistical value which does not fit with the rest of the data.

p

parallel lines are said to be parallel when they are at the same angle to one another, and never meet.

parallelogram a quadrilateral with two pairs of equal and opposite parallel sides.

percentage out of 100.

perimeter distance around the outside of a 2D shape.

perpendicular at 90° to.

pi (π) the ratio between the diameter of a circle and its circumference, approx. 3.142

pictogram a frequency diagram in which a picture or symbol is used to represent a particular frequency.

pie chart a circular diagram divided into sectors to represent data, where the angle at the centre is proportional to the frequency.

place value indicates the value of the digit depending on its position in the number.

position to term a rule which describes how to find a term from its position in a sequence.

positive greater than zero.

power see *index*.

prime a number with exactly two factors, itself and 1.

prism a 3D shape with uniform cross-section.

probability the likeliness of an outcome happening in a given event.

probability scale a scale to measure how likely something is to happen, running from 0 (impossible) to 1 (certain).

product multiplication.

protractor a piece of equipment used to measure angles.

Pythagoras' Theorem in a right-angled triangle, the square on the hypotenuse is equal to the sum of the squares of the other two sides.

q

quadratic based on square numbers.

quadratic equations equations where the highest power of x is x^2.

quadrilateral a four-sided 2D shape.

quantity an amount.

r

radius half the diameter, the measurement from the centre of a circle to the edge.

range the difference between the biggest and smallest number in a set of data.

ratio a comparison of two amounts.

raw data original data as collected.

ray a line connecting corresponding vertices.

reflection a mirror image.

regular polygon a 2D shape that has equal length sides and angles.

rotation a turn.

rounding a number can be rounded (approximated) by writing it to a given number of decimal places or significant figures.

s

sample space a way in which the outcomes of an event are shown.

scale the ratio between two or more quantities.

scale factor the number by which a shape/number has been increased or decreased.

scatter graph paired observations plotted on a 2D graph.

sector a section of a circle enclosed between an arc and two radii (a pie piece).

sequence a set of numbers or shapes which follow a given rule or pattern.

share to divide.

significant figures the importance of digits in a number relative to their position; in 3456 the two most significant figures are 3 and 4.

similar two shapes that have the same shape but not the same size.

simplify make simpler, normally by cancelling a fraction or ratio or by collecting like terms.

simultaneous equations equations that represent lines that intersect.

sin the ratio of the opposite side to the hypotenuse in a right-angled triangle.

solve work out the value of.

speed how fast something is moving.

square a regular polygon; to multiply by itself.

square number a number made from multiplying an integer by itself.

square root the opposite of squaring. A number when multiplied by itself gives the original number.

standard form   a way of writing a large or small number using powers of 10, e.g. $120\,000 = 1.2 \times 10^5$.

substitute   to replace a letter in an expression with a number.

sum   addition.

surface area   the total surface area of all the faces of a 3D shape.

survey   a set of questions used to collect information or data.

t

tan   the ratio of the opposite side to the adjacent side in a right-angled triangle.

term to term   the rule which describes how to move between consecutive terms.

tessellation   a pattern made by repeating 2D shapes with no overlap or gap.

trapezium   a quadrilateral with just one pair of parallel sides.

trial and improvement   try different values to get a more accurate answer.

triangle   a three-sided 2D shape.

u

units   these define length, speed, time, volume, etc.

unlikely   a word used to describe a probability which is between evens and impossible on a probability scale.

v

vertex   the point where the edges meet on a 3D shape.

volume   the capacity, or space, inside a 3D shape.

Index

Notes

Collins

KS3 Revision

Maths

Advanced

Maths

Advanced

KS3

Workbook

**Samya Abdullah, Rebecca Evans
and Gillian Spragg**

Contents

KS3 Maths Workbook

Contents

Number

PS **1** a) Two numbers multiply to make −20. They add to make 1. What are the two numbers?

_____ and _____ [1]

b) Two numbers multiply to make −20, but add to make −1. What are the two numbers?

_____ and _____ [1]

PS **2** Melanie bakes 24 milk chocolate cookies and 30 chocolate chip cookies for a school charity bake sale. She puts the cookies into boxes that each contain the same number of each kind of cookie and uses as many cookies as possible. How many boxes does she need?
Show your working.

_____ boxes [2]

PS **3** a) Put brackets in the calculation to make the answer 60.

$$5 + 4 \times 7 - 3 = 60$$ [1]

b) Put brackets in the calculation to make the answer −10.

$$2 + 3 \times 5 - 7 = -10$$ [1]

4 Complete the table to show the inverse operation. The first one has been done for you.

Operation	Inverse operation
Add 2	Subtract 2
Subtract 7	
Multiply by 6	
Divide by 4	
Square 7	

[4]

Total Marks _____ / 10

(MR) **1** Arjun is thinking of a number. His number is a multiple of 6. Tick the statement which is true.

Arjun's number must be even. ☐

Arjun's number must be odd. ☐

Arjun's number could be odd or even. ☐

Explain your answer.

_____

_____ [2]

2 132 can be written in the form $2^x \times 3 \times 11$. 48 can be written in the form $2^y \times 3$.

x and y are positive integers.

a) Find the value of both x and y.

$x =$ _____ [1]

$y =$ _____ [1]

b) P, Q and R are three different prime numbers. Find the lowest common multiple of the two expressions.

P^2R^3Q and P^3R^2Q

_____ [1]

(MR) **3** Macy says that a cube number multiplied by another cube number will always be positive. Is this statement true or false? Tick the correct answer.

True ☐   False ☐

Explain your answer.

_____

_____ [2]

Total Marks _____ / 7

Sequences

1 Sarah is organising a gala night and needs to seat 50 people. She is planning to use tables which seat six people, as shown below.

However, Sarah realises when she joins the tables together that they no longer seat six people per table, as shown below.

Sarah works out that she can seat 10 people on two tables and 14 people on three tables.

a) Work out how many tables Sarah needs to seat 50 people.

_____ tables [2]

b) If n represents the number of tables, write down a rule that Sarah could use to work out the number of people that can be seated.

_____ [2]

2 **a)** Find the nth term for this sequence of numbers.

5, 7, 9, 11, 13, _____ [2]

b) Ming thinks this is a geometric sequence. Is she correct? Explain your answer.

_____

_____ [2]

3 **a)** Write down the first five terms in the sequence $3n + 2$.

_____ [2]

b) Write down the term-to-term rule.

_____ [1]

Total Marks _____ / 11

(MR) **1** The nth term of a sequence is $4n - 2$.

    a) Work out the 6th term in the sequence.

    .... [2]

    b) The number 56 is one of the terms of this sequence.

        Is this statement true? Tick the correct answer.

        True ☐   False ☐

        Give a reason to justify your answer.

    ....

    .... [2]

    c) The nth term of a different sequence of numbers is $25n^2$. $=(5n)^2$

        Every term in this sequence will be a square number.

        Is this statement true? Tick the correct answer.

        True ☑   False ☐

        Give a reason to justify your answer.

    ....

    .... [2]

2   **a)** Find the nth term for this sequence of numbers.

       2, 5, 10, 17, 26, 37, $n^2 + 1$

    .... [2]

    b) Find the 12th term of the sequence.

    .... [1]

Total Marks .... / 9

Perimeter and Area

(MR) **1** Tomiwa and Joe are working out the area of this circle.

Tomiwa thinks the area of the circle is 12π. Joe thinks the area of the circle is 36π. Who is wrong? Explain why.

....

.... **[2]**

2 The diagram shows the dimensions of a baseball field. Work out the area of the field.

.... m² **[3]**

3 John is painting the top of his garden table with a protective varnish. The table is rectangular with a width of 40cm and length of 60cm.

a) Work out the size of the area which needs to be painted. Give your answer in metres squared.

.... **[2]**

b) A single tin of paint covers 0.15m². Work out how many tins John will need.

.... **[2]**

Total Marks .... / 9

1 Sebastian is designing his new garden.

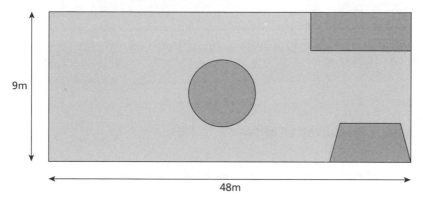

9m

48m

He wants to include the following items in his garden.

0.7m

2m

Shed

0.6m

0.7m

1.5m

Rabbit run

1.5m

Pond

Handwritten working:

$9 \times 48 = 432$

$Shed = 0.7 \times 2 = 1.4$

Rabbit run
$= \frac{1}{2}(0.6 + 1.5) \times 0.7$
$= 0.735$

$Pond = \pi r^2$
$= 3.14 \times 1.5^2$
$= 7.065$

Work out the area of grass Sebastian will have in his garden.

_____ m² [4]

2 Lynne has a new circular table with a radius of 75cm. She wants to make a table cloth to cover it which overhangs the table by 20cm.

a) How much fabric will Lynne need to cover the table? Give your answer in metres squared to 1 decimal place.

_____ m² [3]

b) The fabric she has chosen is only available in rolls of width 2 metres, but she can buy any length. How much fabric she will need to buy? Give your answer in metres squared.

_____ m² [2]

c) How much fabric will be wasted?

_____ m² [2]

Total Marks _____ / 11

Statistics and Data

1 a) Find the median of these numbers.

| 5 | 4 | 7 | 3 | 2 | 5 | 5 |

.... [1]

   b) This card is added to the cards above.

| 8 |

   Does this change the median? Explain your answer.

   ....

   .... [1]

2 a) Calum carries out a survey to find out the most popular choice of music. Complete the table to show his results.

	Rock	Pop	Classical	Total
Male	18			40
Female			6	
Total		42	13	80

[2]

   b) Complete the statements below to help Calum interpret his results. The first one has been done for you.

   ____More____ women preferred ____pop____ than men.

   _____ men preferred _____ than women.

   _____ was _____ popular than _____. [2]

3 Look at the data.

   6, 6, 6, 8, 8, 8, 9, 9, 10, 11, 12, 15

   a) Kirstin thinks the mode is 6, but Dariush says the mode is 8. Who is right?

   Kirstin [ ]   Dariush [ ]   Both of them [ ] [1]

   b) What term is used to describe this situation? .... [1]

   Total Marks .... / 8

1 Jane works out that the mean of seven numbers is 4.4 to 1 decimal place. She realises she has missed a number off the list. The number is 7. Without calculating the new mean, tick the statement which is true when the 8th number is added.

☐ The mean will go up. ☐ The mean will go down. ☐ The mean will stay the same.

Give a reason to justify your answer.

_____

_____ [2]

(PS) 2 The table shows the number of siblings the pupils in Jieun's class have.

Number of siblings	Frequency
0	1
1	10
2	
3	4

The mean number of siblings in the class is 1.8. Fill in the missing frequency. [3]

(PS) 3 The mean of this set of numbers is 5. ☐ $x - 2$ ☐ $2x$ ☐ $x + 2$ ☐ $x + 5$

a) Find the value of x.

_____ [3]

b) Write down the median in terms of x.

_____ [2]

4 Amber is testing the mathematical ability of her classmates. She gives each of them a puzzle and writes down how long it takes them to complete it in minutes. The data is shown in the table.

Time (minutes)	Frequency
0–7	6
8–15	10
16–25	18
26–35	9

Estimate the mean time taken to complete the puzzle. Give your answer to 2 decimal places.

_____ [4]

Total Marks _____ / 14

Decimals

1 Pair each number on the left with a number on the right to make a **product** of 2.

4	0.2
10	0.5
8	0.25
100	0.02

[2]

2 $345.6 \div 1.5$ is the same as $3456 \div 15$. Is this statement true? Tick the correct answer.

True ☐   False ☐

Give a reason to justify your answer.

....

.... [2]

3 Kitchen roll is sold in packs of three and packs of five. A pack of three costs £2.10 and a pack of five costs £3.25.

Which pack gives you better value for money? Show working to justify your answer.

.... [2]

4 a) Write these numbers in order from smallest to largest. 🖩

   17.01   17.001   17.91   17.9007

.... [1]

   b) Work out 1701×1791.

.... [1]

   c) Use your answer to part b) to write down the value of 17.01×17.91.

.... [1]

Total Marks .... / 9

(MR) 1   Number A = 4.05×10^{-5} Number B = 40.5×10^{-4}

Tick the statement which is true.

☐   Number A is greater.

☐   Number B is greater.

☐   They are both the same size.

Justify your answer.

_____

_____   [2]

(MR) 2   **a)** 45×10^{-4}

Angus thinks this number is written in standard form. He is wrong. Explain why.

_____ [1]

b)   Write the number in standard form.

_____ [1]

c)   Work out $(5 \times 10^5) \times (7 \times 10^3)$. Give your answer as an ordinary number.

_____ [1]

d)   Write your answer to part c) in standard form.

_____ [1]

3   Estimate the calculation 21.745 + 8.34

_____ [1]

4   26.12 has been rounded to 2 decimal places. Using an inequality, express the potential rounding error.

_____ [1]

Total Marks _____ / 8

1 Look at the expressions. Work out the value of each expression when $z = 2$.

$4z + 1$ $7 + z^3$ $3z^2 - 5$

....   [2]

2 a) Multiply out the expression. Write your answer as simply as possible.

$2(v + 1) + 4(v - 2)$

....   [2]

b) Factorise $3x^3 - 6x^2$

....   [2]

3 a) Find the value of the expression when $x = 2$ and $y = 3$.

$2xy - 6x^2$

....   [1]

b) Amy works out the value of the expression in part a) when $x = 4$ and $y = 5$. She also works out the value of the expression below when $x = 4$ and $y = 5$. She gets the same answer for both.

$2x(y - 3x)$

Will these two expressions always give the same answer? Give a reason for your answer.

....

....   [2]

4 Simplify the expression.

$\frac{2}{3}x + \frac{1}{6}x$

....   [2]

Total Marks .... / 11

(MR) **1** One of these expressions will give the same answer when $z = 2$ and when $z = -2$.

$4z + 1$ $\qquad\qquad$ $7 + z^3$ $\qquad\qquad$ $3z^2 - 5$

    a) Circle this expression. [1]

    b) Give a reason to justify your answer.

    ....

    .... [1]

2 **a)** Multiply out the expression. Write your answer as simply as possible.

    $(x + 3)(x + 2)$

    .... [2]

    b) Factorise $x^2 + 2x + 1$

    .... [2]

3 $dc = 15$ $\qquad\qquad\qquad$ $dc^2 = 45$

    a) Work out the value of c.

    .... [1]

    b) Work out the value of d.

    .... [1]

4 **a)** Factorise $x^2 + 7x + 10$

    .... [1]

    b) Hence simplify $\dfrac{x^2 + 7x + 10}{x + 2}$

    .... [1]

Total Marks .... / 10

3D Shapes: Volume and Surface Area

1 Calculate the surface area and the volume of each of the cylinders.

A

7cm

6cm

B

4cm

25cm

Surface area: _____

Surface area: _____

Volume: _____

Volume: _____   **[8]**

(PS) 2 What is the height of a cuboid if its volume is 64cm³, its length is 8cm and its width is 4cm?

_____   **[2]**

(PS) 3 What is the radius of a cylinder that has a volume of 1357.2m³ and a length of 12m?

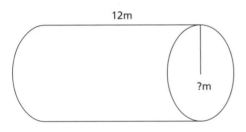

12m

?m

_____   **[2]**

(MR) 4 Joseph is buying fruit juice. He has to choose between these two different containers which cost the same. To get the most juice for his money, which one will he choose?

12cm

15cm

Container A

10cm

12cm

12cm

12cm

Container B

_____   **[4]**

1 What is the surface area and volume of the triangular prism?

5cm

3cm

11cm

4cm

Surface area: _____ Volume: _____ [4]

2 What is the volume of the compound shape?

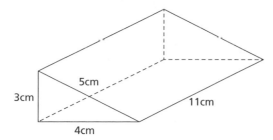

20cm

30cm

24cm 6cm

Volume: _____ [3]

3 This cuboid has a circular hole cut all the way through it. What is the volume of the remaining solid?

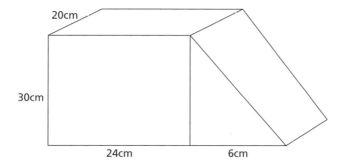

15cm

Radius = 4cm

5cm

18cm

Volume: _____ [3]

4 If a cube has a volume of 125m³, what are its dimensions?

_____ [2]

Total Marks _____ / 12

Interpreting Data

1 540 people were asked what their favourite sweets were. Complete the table and draw a pie chart to show the data.

Category	Frequency	Angle
Polo Mints	55	
Wine Gums	136	
Gummi Bears	124	
Others		

[3]

[2]

2 The graph shows Gareth and Rachel's lemonade sales during a week.

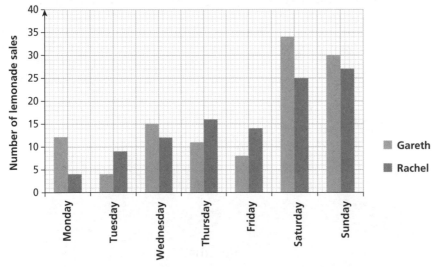

a) On what day was the largest difference between Rachel and Gareth's sales?

....

[2]

b) What was the range of Rachel's sales?

....

[1]

c) What is similar and different between Gareth's and Rachel's lemonade sales?

....

.... [4]

3 Design a question with response box options to find out whether pupils attend the gym more in January than other times of the year.

....

.... [3]

Total Marks .... / 15

1 36 people were asked how they travelled to school. Design a chart to display the following results.

Walking	Cycling	Lift in Car	Bus	Other	Total
14	2	11	8	1	36

[3]

2 a) What type of graph is this?

.... [1]

b) What type of correlation can we see?

.... [1]

c) Describe in a sentence what relationship is shown.

.... [2]

Number of revision sessions attended (vertical axis)

Exam mark (horizontal axis)

Total Marks .... / 7

Fractions

1 Find the missing values:

a) $\frac{?}{12} = 2\frac{5}{12}$ ....

b) $3\frac{5}{9} = \frac{?}{9}$ ....

c) $\frac{6}{?} = 3$ .... [3]

2 Solve and completely simplify:

a) $\frac{5}{7} + \frac{1}{14} =$ ....

b) $\frac{4}{9} + \frac{3}{12} =$ ....

c) $\frac{2}{5} + \frac{10}{25} =$ ....

d) $\frac{6}{7} - \frac{3}{14} =$ ....

e) $\frac{14}{15} - \frac{3}{5} =$ ....

f) $\frac{9}{10} - \frac{3}{7} =$ .... [6]

3 Solve and completely simplify:

a) $\frac{7}{8} \times \frac{8}{10} =$ ....

b) $\frac{1}{4} \times \frac{5}{6} =$ ....

c) $\frac{5}{8} \times \frac{3}{7} =$ ....

d) $\frac{6}{7} \times \frac{1}{3} =$ ....

e) $\frac{1}{2} \times \frac{5}{8} \times \frac{1}{3} =$ ....

f) $\frac{4}{9} \times \frac{2}{5} \times \frac{6}{15} =$ ....

g) $\frac{7}{10} \times \frac{3}{7} \times \frac{4}{9} =$ ....

h) $\frac{4}{5} \div \frac{1}{2} =$ ....

i) $\frac{3}{7} \div \frac{2}{9} =$ ....

j) $\frac{5}{9} \div \frac{3}{11} =$ .... [10]

(MR) 4 Mathew buys a $4\frac{3}{4}$ kg bag of carrots to make two different soups. One recipe requires $2\frac{1}{3}$ kg of carrots and the other $2\frac{1}{7}$ kg of carrots. What fraction of carrots is left over?

.... [3]

(MR) 5 Phil has a jug containing $5\frac{3}{10}$ pints of orange juice. He pours $1\frac{1}{2}$ pints of juice into glasses. What is left in the jug?

.... [3]

(MR) 6 If David has 3 parts of his 14-part train set and Matt lends him 4 parts of his 7-part set, what fraction of a complete 14-part set has David now got?

.... [3]

Total Marks .... / 28

(MR) **1** Martin, the butcher, has $4\frac{1}{2}$ lbs of sausages. He wants to divide the sausages into packs weighing $\frac{9}{10}$ lb. How many packs can Martin make?

_____ [2]

2 Sally spends $\frac{1}{4}$ of her money on transport each month and $\frac{2}{5}$ on rent.

a) What fraction does Sally spend on transport and rent altogether?

_____ [2]

b) What fraction of her money does she have left after paying for transport and rent?

_____ [2]

(FS) **3** Leanne spends $\frac{2}{7}$ of her pocket money on music downloads. She also spends $\frac{1}{5}$ of her money on sweets and keeps £3.60. How much pocket money does Leanne get?

_____ [3]

4 Rhian makes three cakes and splits them equally between Ben and Azim. Ben then splits his into five equal pieces and Azim splits his into seven equal pieces to share. What fraction are Ben and Azim's pieces?

_____

_____

_____ [5]

(FS) **5** Saanvi has £30 from her Granny. She decides to save $\frac{1}{3}$ of it, give $\frac{1}{5}$ of it to charity and spend £3.50 on sweets. How much money has Saanvi got left?

_____

_____

_____ [3]

Total Marks _____ / 17

Coordinates and Graphs

1 **a)** Complete the table for the graph $y = 2x - 1$.

x	−1	0	1	2	3	4
y						

[3]

b) What is the gradient and intercept of this graph?

_____ [2]

c) Plot the graph.

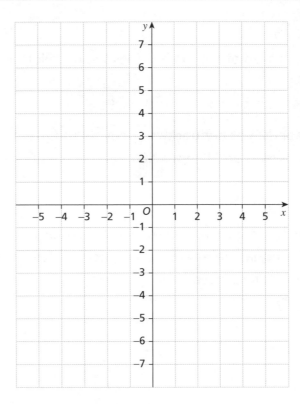

[2]

(MR) **2** **a)** Find another equation which is parallel to the graph $y = 3x + 2$.

_____ [1]

b) Give a pair of coordinates that $y = 3x + 2$ passes through.

_____ [1]

c) Is the equation $3x = y - 8$ parallel to the equation in part a)? Explain your answer.

_____

_____ [1]

Total Marks _____ / 10

1 Complete the table and then plot the graph $y = x^2 + 2x - 5$.

x	−4	−3	−2	−1	0	1	2	3	4
y									

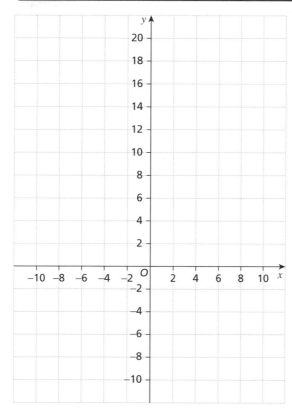

[5]

2 Circle the two equations that are parallel.

a) $y = 3x + 6$ **b)** $y = 7x + 3$ **c)** $y = 5 - 3x$

d) $y = 4x + 3$ **e)** $y = 3x - 9$ [2]

3 Rearrange the following equation into the form $y = ax + b$.

$8x = 2y + 10$

[2]

Total Marks _____ / 9

Angles

1 Complete the table.

Number of sides	Name of shape	Sum of interior angles
3		
	Pentagon	
6		
9		

[4]

(MR) 2 Find the missing angles.

a)

.... [2]

b)

.... [2]

c)

.... [2]

d)

.... [2]

3 Using a pair of compasses, bisect the following angles, showing your construction lines.

a)   b)

[6]

Total Marks .... / 18

1 If a regular polygon has an interior angle of 150°, how many sides does the polygon have?

150°

.... [2]

2 Use a separate sheet of paper for this question. Using a ruler, protractor and pencil, construct a regular pentagon with sides of 5cm. [2]

3 Find the missing angle and explain the reason for your answer.

55°

?°

....

.... [2]

4 A regular shape has an exterior angle of 45° at one corner.

a) What is the name of the shape?

.... [2]

b) What is the interior angle of one corner?

.... [2]

Total Marks .... / 10

Probability

1 Jenny has a bag containing 7 purple sweets and 13 green sweets.

   a) What is the probability that she pulls out a purple sweet?

   _____ [1]

   b) What is the probability that she does not pull out a purple sweet?

   _____ [1]

2 The table shows the probability of Hayley's mum giving her a certain lunch.

   a) Complete the table.

Ham sandwich	Cheese sandwich	Chicken wrap	Other
0.3	0.25	0.412	

[1]

   b) What is the probability that Hayley does not get a ham sandwich?

   _____ [1]

3 Richard has a multipack of crisps containing three bags of cheese and onion, three salt and vinegar, five ready salted and one prawn cocktail. He picks a bag at random.

   a) What is the probability that he takes a salt and vinegar bag?

   _____ [1]

   b) If Richard takes a ready salted bag, what is the probability he will take a bag of prawn cocktail next time?

   _____ [1]

4 Ben is devising a game for his school fair. He has a spinner and a board. On the board are eight segments with either 'winner' or 'loser' on each. The game costs 10p per spin and there is a 20p prize if the spinner lands on a winning segment. How many winning segments should Ben make in order to raise money? Give a reason for your answer.

_____

_____

[3]

1 Darren spins his three-sided spinner. The probability that it will land on A is 0.45 and the probability it will land on B is 0.312. What is the probability it will land on C?

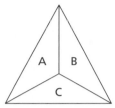

....

[2]

2 **a)** A dice is rolled 100 times and recorded in the frequency table. Complete the table.

Number	Frequency	Estimated probability
1	10	
2	12	
3	24	
4	30	
5	14	
6	10	
	Total	

[3]

b) Use the data in the table to estimate the probability (as decimals) of getting:

i) the number 3 ....

ii) an odd number ....

iii) a number bigger than 4. .... [3]

c) Do you think this dice is fair? Give a reason for your answer.

....

....

.... [2]

Total Marks .... / 10

Fractions, Decimals and Percentages

(PS) **1** A certain bacterium grows in number by 10% each day. At midday on Monday there are 50 000 bacteria. How many bacteria will there be: 🔢

a) at midday on Tuesday?

.... [2]

b) at midday on Wednesday?

.... [2]

(PS)
(MR) **2** Anna scored 38 out of 50 in an English test. Ben scored 32 out of 40. Who got the highest percentage?

.... [2]

(MR) **3** Jane got 18 out of 20 in a Maths test. Aditya took the same test and got 85%. Who did the best in the Maths test? Show your working out.

.... [2]

(FS) **4** John invests £500 in a building society. He receives 4% simple interest per year.

a) How much will John have at the end of 1 year?

.... [2]

b) How much will John have at the end of 3 years?

.... [2]

(PS) **5** A house increases in value from £80 000 to £84 000.

By what percentage does the house increase in value?

.... [3]

Total Marks .... / 15

(PS) **1** What percentage of 3.75kg is 240g?

_____ [2]

(MR) **2** Anya says that if $\frac{1}{10} = 0.1$, then $\frac{1}{8} = 0.8$

a) Is she right?

_____ [1]

b) Give a reason for your answer.

_____

_____ [1]

(MR) **3** Place the numbers in order of size starting with the smallest. 🖩

0.22   25% $\frac{12}{50}$ $\frac{30}{100}$ 20%   0.28

_____ [2]

(PS) **4** A house increases in value by 25% to £120 000.

What was the value of the house **before** the increase?

_____ [3]

(FS) **5** A car is sold for £1700 at a loss of 15%.

What was the original price of the car?

_____ [3]

(PS) **6** Convert the fraction into a percentage.

$\frac{3x}{20}$

_____ [1]

Total Marks _____ / 13

Equations

(PS) **1** I think of a number, subtract 3 and then multiply the result by 7. My answer is the same as multiplying my number by 4 and then adding 3.

What number am I thinking of?

.... [3]

2 Solve these equations. Show your working. 🖩

a) $7y - 4 = 2y + 31$ **b)** $8a + 5 = 3a + 20$ **c)** $7p + 4 = 4p - 2$

.... [6]

(PS) **3** Solve these more complex equations. 🖩

a) $4(2x - 1) = 36$ .... [2]

b) $3x + 8 = 4 - 5x$ .... [2]

c) $\frac{3x - 6}{4} = 3$ .... [2]

d) $\frac{x}{2} + 3 = \frac{x}{4} + 5$ .... [3]

(PS) **4** The perimeter of this rectangle is 56cm. Work out the value of x. 🖩

$3x - 2$

$2x$

.... [3]

Total Marks .... / 21

1 The equation $x^3 - 5x = 170$ has a solution between 5 and 6. Use the table to find the solution to 2 decimal places.

x	x^3	$5x$	$x^3 - 5x$	Too big/too small
5	125	25	100	Too small
6				

$x = $ _____ (2 d.p.) [4]

(PS) **2** Solve the equation.

$5 - \dfrac{6}{3x + 1} = 4$

_____ [3]

3 Solve the equation.

$\dfrac{4}{3x - 2} = \dfrac{3}{2x - 1}$

_____ [3]

(PS) **4** Solve this equation by factorisation.

$x^2 + 9x - 10 = 0$

_____ [4]

Total Marks _____ / 14

1 Complete the following shapes so that they have rotational symmetry of order 4.

a)

b)

c)

[3]

2

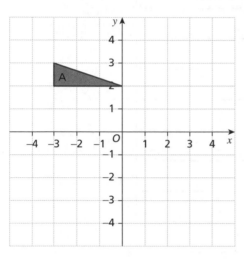

a) Draw the reflection of shape A across the *y*-axis. Label the image B. [1]

b) Reflect shape B across the *x*-axis. Label the image C. [1]

c) Rotate shape A 90° clockwise about the point (−3, 2). Label the shape D. [1]

d) Describe the rotation needed to get from shape C back to shape A.

.... [1]

(MR) **3** Look at the four shapes and complete the sentences below.

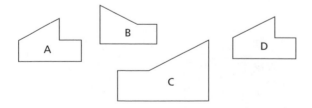

a) Shapes .... and .... are congruent. [1]

b) Shapes .... and .... are similar. [1]

Total Marks .... / 9

1 Enlarge this shape by a scale factor of $\frac{1}{2}$ about the centre of enlargement (–4 , –2).

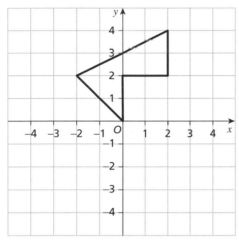

[2]

(MR) **2** Here are two models of the same aeroplane.

The wing span of the larger model is 20cm. What is the wing span of the smaller model?

_____

[2]

(PS) **3** Describe the two transformations that map shape A onto shape C, going via shape B.

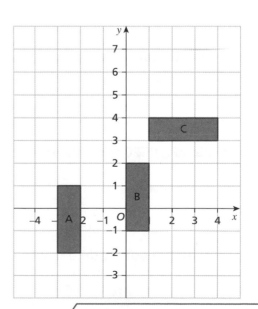

_____

_____

_____

_____

[4]

Total Marks _____ / 8

Ratio and Proportion

PS **1** Simplify the following ratios. 🖩

 a) 35 : 56 ....

 b) £3.60 : £4.20 ....

 c) 40 minutes : 1 hour ....

 d) 16mm : 8cm .... [4]

PS **2** Share 700g of sugar in the ratio 3 : 4. 🖩

.... [2]

FS **3** An amount of money is shared in the ratio 2 : 5. If the smaller share is £16, what is the total amount to be shared?

.... [2]

PS **4** My recipe makes 12 cupcakes. How much of each ingredient will I need to make 30 cupcakes?

Recipe for 12 cupcakes
100g butter
100g caster sugar
100g self-raising flour
$\frac{1}{2}$ teaspoon baking powder
$\frac{1}{2}$ teaspoon vanilla essence
20ml milk
2 eggs

 Butter: ....   Vanilla: ....

 Sugar: ....   Milk: ....

 Flour: ....   Eggs: ....

 Baking powder: ....

[4]

PS **5** The ratio of men to women at a football match is 12 : 5. How many men are there if 3000 women attend the match? 🖩

.... [2]

FS **6** John is paid £25.20 for 6 hours' work in the supermarket.

 a) How much would John be paid for working 8 hours?

.... [2]

 b) How long would it take him to earn £63?

.... [2]

Total Marks .... / 18

FS **1** Ann works as a waitress. Each week she splits her wages into savings and spending money in the ratio 2 : 5.

a) One week, she earns £140. How much does she save that week?

_____ [2]

b) The following week, Ann saves £52. How much does she earn that week?

_____ [2]

FS **2** If 8 pencils cost £2, how much will 3 pencils cost? 🧮

_____ [2]

MR **3** Decide whether the following are examples of direct or inverse proportion. Place each letter in the correct box.

A: The number of pens bought and the cost of the pens

B: The distance travelled and the amount of fuel left in the tank

C: The age of a car and the cost of the car

D: The time you spend on your maths homework and the mark you get for it

Direct proportion	Inverse proportion

[2]

PS **4** Concrete is made from cement, sand and gravel in the ratio $x : 2x : x + 3$. 🧮

How much sand is needed to make 42kg of concrete?

_____ [3]

Total Marks _____ / 11

Real-Life Graphs and Rates

1 You can use this graph to convert miles into kilometres.

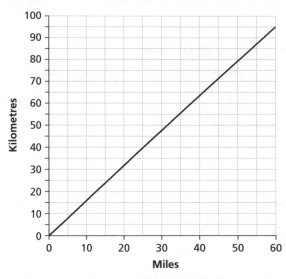

a) Use the graph to estimate how many kilometres are equal to 20 miles.

.... [1]

b) John drives 40 miles to work and Alan drives 60km to work. Who drives the furthest distance? Use the graph to help you.

.... [2]

2 This graph shows Jason's car journey to visit his grandmother.

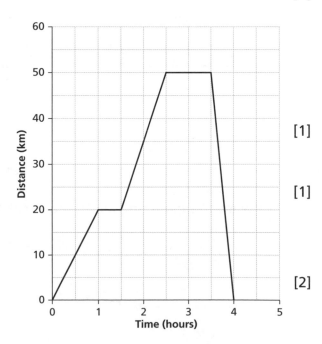

a) How far away does his grandmother live?

.... [1]

b) How long does Jason stop on the journey?

.... [1]

c) Work out Jason's average speed for the whole of his journey (**not** including stops).

.... [2]

Total Marks .... / 7

1 A bus travels at a speed of 30 miles per hour for 2 hours 15 minutes. How far does it travel? Give your answer in miles.

.... [2]

2 A man cycles 5 miles in 12 minutes. What is his speed? Give your answer in miles per hour.

.... [2]

(PS) 3 At 4.40pm Alia sets off in her car to travel to the airport 240km away. She arrives there at 8pm.

Calculate her average speed in miles per hour.

.... [4]

(FS) 4 A pair of jeans costing £75 in the UK costs €80 in Spain. If £1 = €1.25, work out:

a) in which country the jeans are cheapest

.... [2]

b) how much cheaper they are.

.... [1]

5 Calculate the density of this gold bar which is in the shape of a cuboid and has a mass of 350kg.

20cm
80cm
25cm

.... [3]

(FS) 6 On a flight home from Spain, Frank pays £8.20 for two drinks. He is given €2.20 change from a £10 note.

What is the exchange rate from £ to €?

.... [2]

Total Marks .... / 16

1   Use Pythagoras' Theorem to work out the values of p and q. Give your answers to 1 decimal place.

a)

b)

[4]

2   Which of the following triangles are right-angled? Give reasons for your answers.

[3]

3   Work out the length of the side marked y.

[3]

4   Find the value of the following to 2 decimal places.

a) 5 sin 10° _____ (2 d.p.)   [1]

b) 20 cos 34° _____ (2 d.p.)   [1]

c) $\dfrac{15}{\tan 35°}$ _____ (2 d.p.)   [1]

5 Work out the value of x. Give your answers to 1 decimal place.

a)

_____ (1 d.p.)

b)

_____ (1 d.p.) [2]

Total Marks _____ / 15

1 A ramp (AB) extends from an underground garage to street level. The ramp is 25m long and makes an angle of 16° with the horizontal.

a) Calculate the height (BC) of the street level above the base of the garage.

_____ [2]

b) Planners want to increase the incline of the ramp to 21° but keep the height the same.

   i) How long will the ramp be?

   _____ [2]

   ii) How far from C will the ramp have to start?

   _____ [2]

2 Write an expression in terms of x for the vertical height of the triangle.

_____ [4]

Total Marks _____ / 10

No Calculator Allowed

1 Marissa logs how many emails she receives each day for 20 days. She records the data in a stem-and-leaf diagram.

0	4	4	7			
1	3	3	7	7	9	
2	5	5	7	8	8	8
3	1	1	5	7		
4	0	6				

a) Where **2 | 5 = 25**, what is the mode number of Marissa's emails?

....

b) What is the median?

....

c) What other values can you calculate from the diagram?

....

4 marks

2

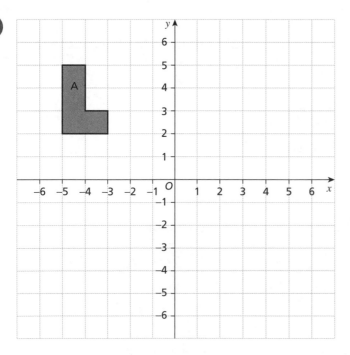

a) Reflect shape A across the *x*-axis.

b) Enlarge shape A by a scale factor 3 from the point (–6 , 5).

c) Rotate shape A 180° from (0 , 0).

5 marks

3 **a)** Plot the equation $y = -x$ on the graph.

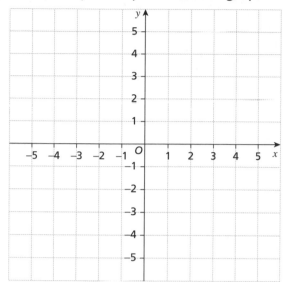

b) Plot these coordinates on the graph.

(2 , 5) (1 , 1)

c) Create an isosceles triangle by finding a third coordinate in the positive quadrant of the axis above.

....

5 marks

4 David has a bag containing different coloured counters: 3 black, 4 red and 8 purple.

a) What is the probability that David will pull out a purple counter?

....

b) What is the probability that he will not pull out a black counter?

....

c) If David pulls out a red counter and leaves it out, what is the probability that he will pull out another red counter?

....

4 marks

TOTAL

18

5 Put the cards into three sets that give the same value.

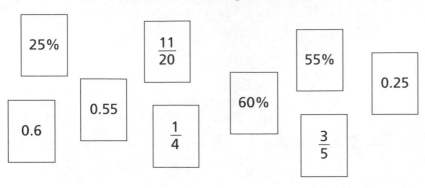

Set 1: _____ = _____ = _____

Set 2: _____ = _____ = _____

Set 3: _____ = _____ = _____

3 marks

6 This is an isosceles triangle. The perimeter of the triangle is $5a + 4b$.

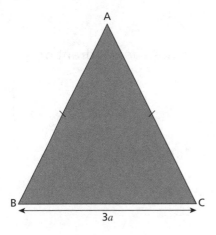

a) Find an expression in terms of a and b for the length of side AB.

_____

b) Given that the value of a is 6 and the perimeter is 62, find the value of b.

_____

7 Which of the following equations does not give the same answer as the others?

| **A:** $13 + 2p = 21$ | **B:** $p - 5 = -2$ | **C:** $5p - 13 = 7$ | **D:** $\frac{32}{2p} = 4$ |

_____

4 marks

1 mark

8 The table shows some percentages of amounts of money.

	£10	£40	£65
10%	£1	£4	£6.50
5%	50p	£2	£3.25

Use the table to complete the following.

a) 15% of £65 = ...

b) £1.50 = 15% of ....

c) £14 = ... of £40

d) £1 = 5% of ....

4 marks

9 Look at the calculation.

$5^2 + 10^2 = 5^x$

Find the value of x.

....

2 marks

10 Translate this shape by vector $\begin{pmatrix} -3 \\ 2 \end{pmatrix}$.

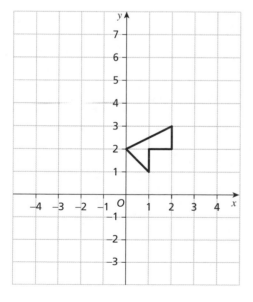

2 marks

TOTAL

16

Mixed Test-Style Questions

11 Sally wants to buy 12 calculators. Two shops have different offers on calculators.

Calcs R Us	ABC Calcs
All calculators	All calculators
15% off	£7.50 each
Normal price £7	Buy 2, get 1 free

In which shop will Sally pay the least for her calculators?

....

4 marks

12 The length of a rectangle is 6cm more than its width. The perimeter of the rectangle is 40cm. Work out the width.

....

3 marks

13 Over the course of a week, Richard eats $\frac{3}{8}$ of a cake and Sally eats $\frac{1}{5}$. How much is left for Joan?

....

2 marks

14 **a)** Work out the size of the largest angle in the triangle.

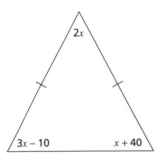

....

b) What is the special name given to this triangle?

....

4 marks

15 The first four terms of a sequence are 4, 10, 20 and 34.

For each expression in the table, put a cross if it cannot be the nth term for this sequence or a tick if it could be the nth term. If you put a tick, work out the 5th term in the sequence. The first one has been done for you.

Expression	Could it be the nth term?	5th term
$3n + 1$	✗	
$2(n^2 + 1)$		
$n + 6$		
$2n^2 + 2$		

3 marks

16 **a)** Give an example which contradicts this statement.

When you multiply a number by 4, the answer is always greater than 4.

b) Give an example which contradicts this statement.

When you divide a number by 4, the answer is always less than the number itself.

c) Is this statement true for all numbers?

The cube of a number is always greater than the number itself.

Yes ☐   No ☐

Justify your answer.

3 marks

TOTAL ☐

19

17 A wind farm is to be built off the coast. The wind turbines must be at least 7 miles from the road linking Sandy Bay to Ullsworth.

Mark on the diagram where the wind turbines may be built.

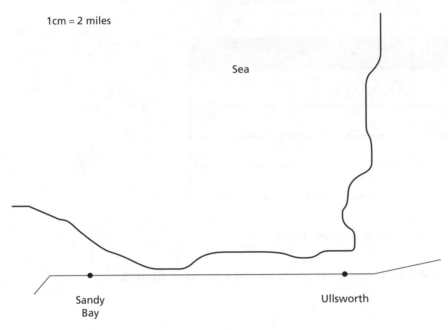

1cm = 2 miles

Sea

Sandy
Bay

Ullsworth

1 mark

18 Work out the missing numbers. In each case, use the first line to help you.

a) $17 \times 15 = 255$

$17 \times$ _____ $= 510$

b) $255 \div 17 = 15$

$255 \div$ _____ $= 30$

c) $35 \div 2 = 17.5$

$35 \times \frac{1}{2} =$ _____

3 marks

19 **a)** Explain why $\sqrt{75}$ must be between 8 and 9.

_____

_____

b) $\sqrt{421}$ is between which two positive consecutive integers?

_____ and _____

3 marks

20 Solve and fully simplify the following:

a) $\frac{3}{7} \times \frac{2}{11} =$ ....

b) $\frac{3}{5} \times \frac{1}{9} =$ ....

c) $\frac{4}{7} \div \frac{1}{8} =$ ....

3 marks

21 Find the missing angles.

a)

.... °

b)

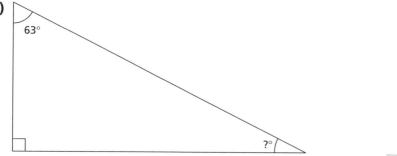

.... °

4 marks

22 a) Draw all the lines of symmetry on the shape.

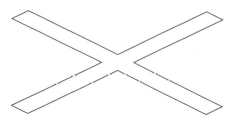

b) What is the order of rotational symmetry of the shape?

....

2 marks

TOTAL

16

Mixed Test-Style Questions

Calculator Allowed

1 Find the volume of the shapes.

a)

350mm

12mm

250mm

Volume = ...

....

.... mm³

b)

46cm

Radius = 14cm

Volume = ...

....

.... cm³

c)

Diameter = 3.2m

0.4m

Volume = ...

....

.... m³   ☐

6 marks

2 Find the missing angles.

a)

105°

?°

.... °

b)

10°

?°

.... °   ☐

4 marks

3 The table gives information about average hours of sunshine per month in three places in Europe (A, B and C).

	Average hours of sunshine per month	Number of months	Months
A	480	7	April–October
	360	5	November–March
B	390	8	March–October
	270	4	November–February
C	420	6	May–October
	450	6	November–April

Which place has more hours of sunshine on average over the whole year?
Tick the correct box and show working to justify your answer.

A ☐   B ☐   C ☐

☐
3 marks

4 Work out $\frac{3}{5}$ of 650cm.

.... cm

☐
2 marks

5 Max is paid a basic rate of £3.60 per hour. The hourly rate for overtime is 40% more. During the week, Max works a basic 40 hours and 5 hours overtime.

a) Calculate the amount he earns in the week.

....

b) Deductions of 30% of his earnings are made for tax and National Insurance contributions. Calculate Max's 'take home' pay.

....

☐
5 marks

TOTAL
☐
20

Mixed Test-Style Questions

6 Mark picks cards at random from a special pack of cards. The frequencies are shown in the table.

Cards	Crowns	Jesters	Castles	Kings	Queens
Frequency	20	15	15	25	25
Probability					

Complete the table by working out the probability (as decimals) of each card being picked out.

3 marks

7 Use Pythagoras' Theorem to work out which triangle does not have a right angle. Tick the correct box.

_____

_____

A ☐   B ☐

_____

_____

C ☐   D ☐

4 marks

8 Solve the equations.

a) $8 + 6x = 56$ b) $7x + 2 = 3x - 10$

_____

2 marks

9 To make orange paint, yellow and red paint are mixed in the ratio 5 : 3.

How much yellow paint would need to be mixed with:

a) 6 litres of red paint? ....

b) 12 litres of red paint? ....

c) 7.5 litres of red paint? ....

3 marks

10 This solid has had a cuboid removed from one side to the other.

What is the volume of the remaining solid?

4.2m

0.8m

0.3m

3.5m

0.5m

Volume = ...

3 marks

11 The Robinsons are travelling to France for their summer holiday. When they leave, the exchange rate is £1 = €1.32.

Mr Robinson changes £500. How many euros will he get?

....

1 mark

12 **a)** Complete the factorisation.

$\frac{1}{4}x + 3$

$\frac{1}{4}(x + ...)$

b) Complete the factorisation.

$2x + 24$

$2(x + ...)$

c) Hence simplify: $\dfrac{\frac{1}{4}x + 3}{2x + 24}$

....

3 marks

TOTAL

19

Mixed Test-Style Questions

13 The graph compares the nutritional values of cookies and shortbread.

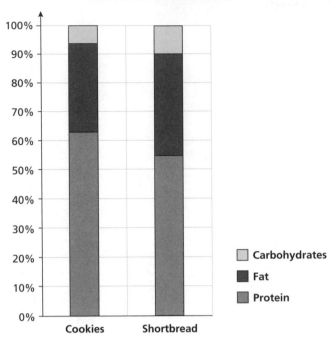

Nutritional values of biscuits

a) Which biscuit contains the most fat? ....

b) How much more fat does it contain? ....

2 marks

14 This isosceles triangle has a base length of 12cm and one angle of 40°.

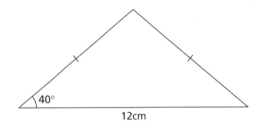

40°

12cm

a) Calculate the vertical height of the triangle.

....

....

b) Calculate the length of one of the equal sides.

....

....

4 marks

15 **a)** Complete the table and plot the graph of $y = 4x - 3$.

x	−3	−2	−1	0	1
y					

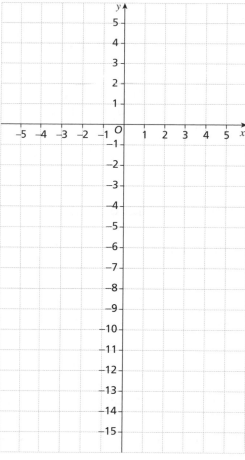

b) What is the y-intercept of the graph $y = x^2 + 8x + 13$?

....

c) What is the gradient of the graph $2y = 14x - 6$?

....

6 marks

16 Solve the equation $3(x + 1) = 2 + 4(2 - x)$.

....

....

....

....

3 marks

TOTAL

15

Mixed Test-Style Questions

17   Here are the ingredients for making 18 rock cakes.

> 9 cups of flour
>
> 6 cups of sugar
>
> 6 cups of butter
>
> 8 cups of dried mixed fruit
>
> 2 large eggs

Mark wants to make 12 rock cakes.

a)   How much sugar does he need?

....

b)   How much dried fruit does he need? Give your answer to the nearest cup.

....

Mark has only 9 cups of butter but has plenty of all the other ingredients.

c)   What is the greatest number of rock cakes he can make?

....

6 marks

18   The graph shows the exchange rate between British pounds (£) and US dollars ($).

a)   How many dollars would you get for:

    i)   £2? ....

    ii)   £10? ....

    iii)   £200?

b)   How many pounds would you get for:

    i) $8? ....

    ii) $40?

5 marks

19 A wire of 22m in length runs from the top of a pole to the ground as shown in the diagram. The wire makes an angle of 35° with the ground.

Calculate the height of the pole. Give your answer to a suitable degree of accuracy.

....

....

2 marks

20 Lewis takes a trip in a hot air balloon. The balloon rises 600m in one hour and stays at this height for two and a half hours. The balloon then comes back to earth in half an hour.

Use the grid to draw a distance–time graph for the balloon flight.

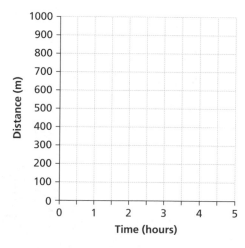

3 marks

21 Calculate the density of:

a) a gold bar with a mass of 350kg and a volume of 0.04m³

....

b) an aluminium block with a mass of 900kg and a volume of 0.2m³.

....

4 marks

TOTAL

20

Mixed Test-Style Questions

22 Wasim works in a charity shop. He records 200 items contained in some donated bags and puts them into the table below.

Item	Frequency	Estimated probability
Clothing	78	
Games	24	
Bric-a-brac	32	
Books	41	
Other	25	

a) Complete the estimated probability for the items.

b) Which is the less likely combination of items, clothing and games or books and bric-a-brac?

....

....

....

c) Using the estimated probability, calculate the number of books Wasim might find after sorting through 500 items.

....

....

....

6 marks

23 Is this pair of triangles congruent? Give your reasons.

....

....

2 marks

TOTAL

8

KS3 Advanced Maths Workbook Answers

Pages 148–149

Number

1. a) −4 and +5 [1]

    Remember: − × + = −

    b) +4 and −5 [1]
2. 6 [2]

    The question is asking you to find the HCF of 24 and 30.

    [2 marks for 6 boxes or both 30 = 2 × 3 × 5 and 24 = 2³ × 3; 1 mark for one of 30 = 2 × 3 × 5 or 24 = 2³ × 3]

    Use a prime factor tree; 2 and 3 are both common factors so the HCF is 6.

3. a) $(5 + 4) \times 7 - 3 = 60$ [1]
    b) $(2 + 3) \times (5 - 7) = -10$ [1]
4.

Operation	Inverse operation
Add 2	Subtract 2
Subtract 7	**Add 7 [1]**
Multiply by 6	**Divide by 6 [1]**
Divide by 4	**Multiply by 4 [1]**
Square 7	**Square root 49 [1]**

1. Arjun's number must be even. [1]
    Any multiple of 6 must also be a multiple of 2 and so will always be even. [1]
2. a) $x = 2$ **[1]** $y = 4$ **[1]**

    Remember to use a prime factor tree.

    b) P^3R^3Q [1]

    Construct a Venn diagram and place common factors in the overlap.

3. False **[1]**, as cube numbers can be positive and negative and a negative multiplied by a positive is a negative. **[1]**

Pages 150–151

Sequences

1. a) 12 tables **[2] [1 mark for 48]**
    b) $4n + 2$ **[2] [1 mark for 4n]**
2. a) $2n + 3$ **[2] [1 mark for 2n]**
    b) No **[1]**, as common difference not common multiple **[1]**
3. a) 5, 8, 11, 14, 17 [2]
    [1 mark for any three correct]
    b) +3 [1]

1. a) 22 **[2] [1 mark for 4 × 6 −2]**
    b) $4n - 2 = 56$, $4n = 58$, $n = 14.5$
       False **[1]**, as not a whole number **[1]**
    c) True **[1]**, it can be written as $(5n)^2$ **[1]**
2. a) $n^2 + 1$ **[2] [1 mark for n²]**
    b) 145 [1]

Pages 152–153

Perimeter and Area

1. Tomiwa is wrong **[1]** – he works out the circumference, not the area. **[1]**
2. 9200m² [3]
    [2 marks for 6000 and 3200 or 10 000 and 800; 1 mark for either 6000 or 3200 or 10 000 or 800]

    Remember that this can be split into a rectangle and trapezium *or* a rectangle minus a triangle.

3. a) 0.24m² **[2] [1 mark for 60 × 40 or 0.6 × 0.4]**
    b) 2 tins **[2] [1 mark for 0.24 ÷ 0.15]**

1. 422.8m^2 [4]

    [3 marks for 432, 1.4, 0.735 and 7.068 583
    471; 2 marks for any two of 432, 1.4, 0.735
    or 7.068 583 471; 1 mark for any one of
    432, 1.4, 0.735 or 7.068 583 471]

    Find the area of the rectangle and then
    subtract the area of the pond, shed and
    rabbit run.

2. a) 2.8m^2 [3]

    [2 marks for $\pi \times 0.95^2$ or $\pi \times 95^2$; 1 mark
    for 0.95, 95, 1.9 or 190]

    b) 3.8m^2 [2] [1 mark for 2×190 *or* 2×1.9]

    c) 1m^2 [2]

    [1 mark for answer from b) minus
    answer from a)]

Pages 154–155
Statistics and Data

1. a) 5 [1]

    Remember to write the numbers in order
    first.

    b) No. The next number in the list is also a
    5 so it will not change. [1]

2. a) Completely correct [2]

    [1 mark for four out of six correct]

	Rock	Pop	Classical	Total
Male	18	15	7	40
Female	7	27	6	40
Total	25	42	13	80

    b) Any correct statement, for example:
    More men preferred **rock** *or* **classical**
    than women. [1]
    Rock was **more** popular than **classical**. [1]
    or:
    Pop was **more** popular than **both rock**
    and **classical**. [1]

3. a) Both [1]

    b) Bimodal [1]

1. The mean will go up [1] because 7 is
    greater than 4.4. [1]

2. 25 [3]

    [2 marks for $2x + 22$ and $x + 15$; 1 mark for
    either $2x + 22$ or $x + 15$. Accept any letter in
    place of x.]

3. a) 3 [3]

    [2 marks for $\dfrac{5x + 5}{4}$; 1 mark for
    $5x + 5$]

    b) $\dfrac{3x + 2}{2}$ or $x + 2.5$ [2]

    [1 mark for 5.5]

4. 18.13 minutes [4]

    [3 marks for $779.5 \div 43$; 2 marks for any three
    of 21, 115, 369, 274.5 as fx; 1 mark for any
    three of 3.5, 11.5, 20.5 or 30.5 as midpoints]

Pages 156–157
Decimals

1. 4 and 0.5; 8 and 0.25; 10 and 0.2; 100 and
    0.02
    All correct [2] [1 mark for two correct]

2. True [1], they are equivalent fractions. [1]

3. Pack of 5 with 70 and 65 *or* 0.70 and
    0.65 [same addition for 1 mark] [2]

4. a) 17.001, 17.01, 17.9007, 17.91 [1]

    b) 3 046 491 [1]

    c) 304.6491 [1]

1. Number B is greater [1] as A = 0.000 040 5
    but B = 0.004 05 [1]

2. a) 45 is not between 1 and 10. [1]

    b) 4.5×10^{-3} [1]

    c) 3 500 000 000 [1]

    d) 3.5×10^9 [1]

3. 22 + 8 = 30 [1]

4. $-0.005 \leqslant x < 0.005$ [1]

Pages 158–159
Algebra

1. 9, 15 and 7 [2] [1 mark for any two correct]

    Remember BIDMAS.

2. a) $6v - 6$ **[2]** [1 mark for $2v + 2 + 4v - 8$ or any three terms correct]

   b) $3x^2(x - 2)$ **[2]**
   [1 mark for $3x(x^2 - 2x)$]

3. a) -12 **[1]**

   b) Yes **[1]**, as the first expression has been factorised to make the second. **[1]**

4. $\frac{5x}{6}$ **[2]** [1 mark for $\frac{4x}{6} + \frac{1x}{6}$]

---

1. a) $3z^2 - 5$ **[1]**

   b) Because $2^2 = (-2)^2$ **[1]**

2. a) $x^2 + 5x + 6$ **[2]**
   [1 mark for $x^2 + 3x + 2x + 6$ or any three terms correct]

   b) $(x + 1)(x + 1)$ or $(x + 1)^2$ **[2]**

3. a) $c = 3$ **[1]**

   b) $d = 5$ **[1]**

4. a) $(x + 2)(x + 5)$ **[1]**

   b) $(x + 5)$ **[1]**

Pages 160–161

3D Shapes: Volume and Surface Area

1. Cylinder A:
   Surface area: $2(7^2 \times \pi) + (14 \times \pi) \times 6 = 571.8\text{cm}^2$ **[2]**
   Volume: $7^2 \times \pi \times 6 = 923.6\text{cm}^3$ **[2]**
   Cylinder B:
   Surface area: $2(2^2 \times \pi) + (4 \times \pi) \times 25 = 339.3\text{cm}^2$ **[2]**
   Volume: $2^2 \times \pi \times 25 = 314.2\text{cm}^3$ **[2]**
   [2 marks for each correct answer; 1 mark for method]

2. $8 \times 4 \times ? = 64$
   $64 \div 32 = 2\text{cm}$ **[2]**
   [2 marks for correct answer; 1 mark for method]

3. $1357.2 \div 12 = 113.1$
   $113.1 \div \pi = 36$
   $\sqrt{36} = 6\text{m}$ **[2]**
   [2 marks for correct answer; 1 mark for method]

4. Container A as the volume is greater.
   Container A: $6^2 \times \pi \times 15 = 1696.5\text{cm}^3$
   Container B: $10 \times 12 \times 12 = 1440\text{cm}^3$ **[4]**
   [1 mark for each method and answer]

---

1. Surface area: $2(3 \times 4 \times \frac{1}{2}) + (5 \times 11) + (3 \times 11) + (4 \times 11) = 144\text{cm}^2$ **[2]**
   Volume: $\frac{1}{2}(3 \times 4) \times 11 = 66\text{cm}^3$ **[2]**
   [2 marks for each correct answer; 1 mark for each method]

2. Volume: $(30 \times 20 \times 24) + (\frac{1}{2} \times 6 \times 30 \times 20) = 16\,200\text{cm}^3$ **[3]**
   [1 mark for the volume of each shape; 1 mark for total]

3. $18 \times 5 \times 15 = 1350$
   $4^2 \times \pi \times 5 = 251.3$
   $1350 - 251.3 = 1098.7\text{cm}^3$ **[3]**
   [1 mark for each part]

4. $\sqrt[3]{125} = 5$, so $5\text{m} \times 5\text{m} \times 5\text{m}$ **[2]**
   [1 mark for cube root; 1 mark for correct answer]

Pages 162–163

Interpreting Data

1.

Category	Frequency	Angle
Polo Mints	55	37°
Wine Gums	136	90°
Gummi Bears	124	83°
Others	225	150°

[3 marks if all correct; 2 marks if three rows correct; 1 mark if two rows correct]

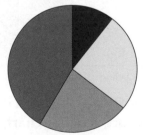

■ Polo Mints □ Wine Gums ▨ Gummi Bears ■ Others

[2 marks if all sectors correct to within 2°; 1 mark if two correct]

> If one angle has to be rounded down to fit into a pie chart, round the largest one so it is the least proportional error.

2. a) Saturday – difference of 9 **[2]**
   b) $27 - 4 = 23$ **[1]**
   c) Sales at the weekend were significantly increased for both. **[1]**
   Both had their least amount of sales on Tuesday. **[1]**
   Rachel outsold Gareth on three days: Tuesday, Thursday and Friday. **[1]**
   Gareth outsold Rachel on four days: Monday, Wednesday, Saturday and Sunday. **[1]**

3. Question must be specific, using a time reference; answer boxes cannot overlap and must cover all options. **[3]**
   [1 mark for each correct part]

1.
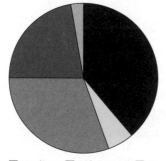

How people travel to school

■ Walking □ Cycling ■ Lift in car ■ Bus ■ Other

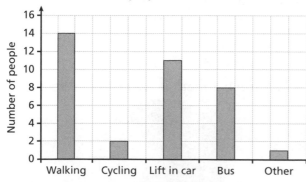

How people travel to school

[3] [1 mark for correct labels; 1 mark for an appropriate chart, e.g. bar chart, pie chart; 1 mark for full correct chart]

2. a) Scatter graph **[1]**
   b) A positive correlation **[1]**

c) The more revision sessions attended **[1]**, the more likely you will achieve a higher exam mark. **[1]**

Pages 164–165
Fractions

1. a) $2 \times 12 + 5 \quad \frac{29}{12}$ **[1]**
   b) $3 \times 9 + 5 \quad \frac{32}{9}$ **[1]**
   c) $\frac{6}{2}$ **[1]**

2. a) $\frac{11}{14}$ **[1]**
   b) $\frac{25}{36}$ **[1]**
   c) $\frac{4}{5}$ **[1]**
   d) $\frac{9}{14}$ **[1]**
   e) $\frac{1}{3}$ **[1]**
   f) $\frac{33}{70}$ **[1]**

3. a) $\frac{7}{10}$ **[1]**
   b) $\frac{5}{24}$ **[1]**
   c) $\frac{15}{56}$ **[1]**
   d) $\frac{2}{7}$ **[1]**
   e) $\frac{5}{48}$ **[1]**
   f) $\frac{16}{225}$ **[1]**
   g) $\frac{2}{15}$ **[1]**
   h) $1\frac{3}{5}$ **[1]**
   i) $1\frac{13}{14}$ **[1]**
   j) $2\frac{1}{27}$ **[1]**

4. $2\frac{1}{3} + 2\frac{1}{7} = 4 + \frac{7}{21} + \frac{3}{21}$ **[1]**
   $4\frac{10}{21}$ **[1]**
   $4\frac{3}{4} - 4\frac{10}{21} = \frac{23}{84}$ **[1]**

5. $5\frac{3}{10} - 1\frac{1}{2}$ **[1]**
   $5\frac{3}{10} - \frac{3}{2}$ **[1]**
   $\frac{19}{5} = 3\frac{4}{5}$ pts **[1]**

6. $\frac{3}{14} + \frac{4}{7} = \frac{3}{14} + \frac{8}{14} = \frac{11}{14}$ **[3]**
   [1 mark for each part]

1. $4\frac{1}{2} \div \frac{9}{10}$ **[1]** $= 5$ **[1]**

2. a) $\frac{1}{4} + \frac{2}{5}$ **[1]** $= \frac{13}{20}$ **[1]**

   b) $1 - \frac{13}{20}$ **[1]** $= \frac{7}{20}$ **[1]**

3. $\frac{2}{7} + \frac{1}{5} = \frac{17}{35}$

   $1 - \frac{17}{35} = \frac{18}{35}$ **[1]**

   $\frac{18}{35} = £3.60$

   $£3.60 \div 18 = 0.2$

   $0.2 \times 35 = £7$ **[2]**

4. $\frac{3}{2} = 1\frac{1}{2}$ **[1]**

   Ben: $1\frac{1}{2} \div 5$ **[1]** $= \frac{3}{2} \div \frac{5}{1} = \frac{3}{2} \times \frac{1}{5} = \frac{3}{10}$ **[1]**

   Azim: $1\frac{1}{2} \div 7$ **[1]** $= \frac{3}{2} \div \frac{7}{1} = \frac{3}{2} \times \frac{1}{7} = \frac{3}{14}$ **[1]**

5. $\frac{1}{3}$ of £30 = £10 savings **[1]**

   $\frac{1}{5}$ of £30 = £6 charity **[1]**

   £30 − 10 − 6 − 3.50 = £10.50 **[1]**

Pages 166–167

Coordinates and Graphs

1. a)

x	−1	0	1	2	3	4
y	−3	−1	1	3	5	7

[3]

   [$\frac{1}{2}$ mark for each correct answer]

   b) gradient = 2 **[1]**, intercept = −1 **[1]**

   c)

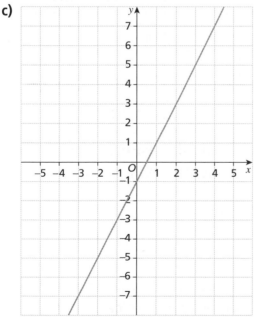

[2]

[1 mark if the graph passes through one correct coordinate]

2. a) $y = 3x + $ (any number) **[1]**

   b) $3x + 2$

x	1	2	3	0	−1	−2	−3
y	5	8	11	2	−1	−4	−7

   [1 mark for any pair of coordinates]

   c) Yes, as it can be rearranged to
   $y = 3x + 8$ **[1]**

1.

x	−4	−3	−2	−1	0	1	2	3	4
y	3	−2	−5	−6	−5	−2	3	10	19

[3 marks if all correct; 2 marks for six correct answers; 1 mark for three correct answers]

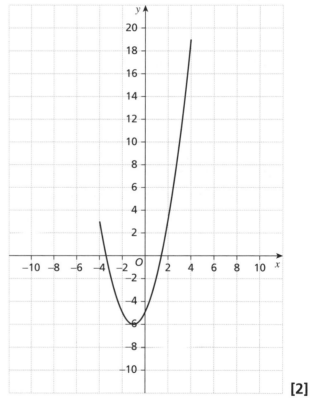

[2]

2. a) and e) are parallel (as they have the same gradient) **[2]**

3. (÷ 2) $4x = y + 5$ **[1]**

   $y = 4x − 5$ **[1]**

Pages 168–169

Angles

1.

Number of sides	Name of shape	Sum of interior angles
3	Triangle	180°
5	Pentagon	540°
6	Hexagon	720°
9	Nonagon	1260°

[4]

[1 mark for each correct full line]

2. a) 180° − 135° = 45° [1]
   180° − 45° − 45° = 90° [1]
   b) 180° − 150° = 30°
   360° − 30° − 30° = 300° [1]
   300° ÷ 2 = 150° [1]
   c) 180° − 73° [1] = 107° [1]
   d) 180° − 54° [1] = 126° [1]

> Corresponding angles, then angles on a straight line add up to 180°

3. [for both a) and b): 1 mark for construction lines on the angle lines; 1 mark for construction cross; 1 mark for bisecting line] [6]

1. Interior angle + exterior angle = 180°
   180° − 150° = 30° [1]
   360° ÷ 30° = 12 [1]

2.

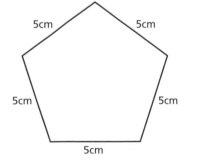

5cm 5cm
5cm 5cm
5cm

[2]

[1 mark for correct angles; 1 mark for correct length of sides]

3. The angle is 55° [1] because in a set of parallel lines with a line going through it alternate angles [1] are equal.

4. a) 360 ÷ 45 = 8 [1], octagon [1]
   b) 180 − 45 [1] = 135° [1]

Pages 170–171

Probability

1. a) $\frac{7}{20}$ [1]
   b) $\frac{13}{20}$ [1]

2. a)

Ham sandwich	Cheese sandwich	Chicken wrap	Other
0.3	0.25	0.412	0.038

[1]

   b) 1 − 0.3 = 0.7 [1]

3. a) $\frac{3}{12} = \frac{1}{4}$ [1]
   b) $\frac{1}{11}$ [1]

4. Possible answer: 4 winning segments give a probability of breaking even [1], so no more than 3 [1], and possibly fewer, should raise more money [1].

1. 1 − (0.45 + 0.312) [1] = 0.238 [1]

2. a)

Number	Frequency	Estimated probability
1	10	0.1
2	12	0.12
3	24	0.24
4	30	0.3
5	14	0.14
6	10	0.1
	Total 100	1

[3 marks if all correct; 2 marks for five correct rows; 1 mark for three correct rows]

   b) i) 0.24 [1]
   ii) 0.1 + 0.24 + 0.14 = 0.48 [1]
   iii) 0.14 + 0.1 = 0.24 [1]

   c) You would expect a more evenly spread frequency if the dice is fair [1], so we can conclude that this dice is likely to be biased. [1]

Pages 172–173

Fractions, Decimals and Percentages

1. a) $10\% = 5000$
$50\,000 + 5000$ **[1]** $= 55\,000$ bacteria **[1]**
b) $10\% = 5500$
$55\,000 + 5500$ **[1]** $= 60\,500$ bacteria **[1]**

2. Anna: $38 \div 50 \times 100 = 76\%$
Ben: $32 \div 40 \times 100 = 80\%$ **[1]**
Ben scored the highest percentage. **[1]**

3. $18 \div 20 \times 100 = 90\%$ **[1]**
Jane did better than Aditya by 5%. **[1]**

4. a) $0.04 \times 500 = 20$ **[1]**
$500 + 20 = £520$ **[1]**
b) $20 \times 3\text{yrs} = £60$ **[1]**
$500 + 60 = £560$ **[1]**

5. The increase in value is £4000. **[1]**
$4000 \div 80\,000 \times 100$ **[1]**
The value increased by 5%. **[1]**

1.
> To compare the quantities, the units must be the same.

$3.75\text{kg} = 3750\text{g}$
$240 \div 3750 \times 100$ **[1]**
$= 6.4\%$ **[1]**

2. a) No **[1]**
b) Because $\frac{1}{8}$ is $1 \div 8 = 0.125$, not 0.8
or Because $0.8 = \frac{4}{5}$ **[1]**

3. 20%   0.22 $\frac{12}{50}$ 25%   0.28 $\frac{30}{100}$

> Change each value into a percentage to compare.

[2 marks for all in correct order; 1 mark for 4 in correct order]

4. $125\% = £120\,000$
$1\% = 120\,000 \div 125 = 960$ **[1]**
$100\% = 960 \times 100$ **[1]**
$= 96\,000$
Value of the house before the increase was £96 000. **[1]**

5. $85\% = £1700$
$1\% = 1700 \div 85 = 20$ **[1]**
$100\% = 20 \times 100$ **[1]**
$= 2000$
Original price of the car was £2000. **[1]**

6. $\frac{3x}{20} = \frac{15x}{100} = 15x\%$ **[1]**

Pages 174–175

Equations

1. $7(n - 3) = 4n + 3$ **[1]**
$7n - 21 = 4n + 3$
$3n - 21 = 3$ **[1]**
$3n = 24$
$n = 8$
I am thinking of the number 8. **[1]**

2. a) $7y - 4 = 2y + 31$
$5y - 4 = 31$ **[1]**
$5y = 35$
$y = 7$ **[1]**
b) $8a + 5 = 3a + 20$
$5a + 5 = 20$ **[1]**
$5a = 15$
$a = 3$ **[1]**
c) $7p + 4 = 4p - 2$
$3p + 4 = -2$ **[1]**
$3p = -6$
$p = -2$ **[1]**

3. a) $4(2x - 1) = 36$

> Expand the brackets first.

$8x - 4 = 36$ **[1]**
$8x = 40$
$x = 5$ **[1]**
b) $3x + 8 = 4 - 5x$
$8x + 8 = 4$ **[1]**
$8x = -4$
$x = -0.5$ **[1]**
c) $\frac{3x - 6}{4} = 3$
$3x - 6 = 12$ **[1]**
$3x = 18$
$x = 6$ **[1]**

d) $\frac{x}{2} + 3 = \frac{x}{4} + 5$

Remember to multiply every term.

$(\times 2)\, x + 6 = \frac{2x}{4} + 10$ **[1]**

$(\times 4)\, 4x + 24 = 2x + 40$ **[1]**

$\qquad\qquad 2x = 16$

$\qquad\qquad\; x = 8$ **[1]**

4. $3x - 2 + 3x - 2 + 2x + 2x = 56\text{cm}$

[1 mark for writing a correct expression]

$10x - 4 = 56\text{cm}$

[1 mark for simplifying the expression]

$10x = 60\text{cm}$

$\quad x = 6\text{cm}$ **[3]**

1.

x	x^3	$5x$	$x^3 - 5x$	Too big/ too small
5	125	25	100	Too small
6	216	30	**186**	**Too big**
5.5	166.375	27.5	**138.875**	**Too small**
5.8	195.112	28	**166.112**	**Too small**
5.9	205.379	29.5	**175.879**	**Too big**
5.85	200.201 625	29.25	**170.951 625**	**Too big**
5.83	198.155 287	29.15	**169.005 287**	**Too small**
5.84	199.176 704	29.2	**169.976 704**	**Too small**
5.845	199.688 72..	29.225	**170.463 7..**	**Too big**

$x = 5.84$ (2 d.p.)   **[4]**

[3 marks for a method similar to the above]

2. $5(3x + 1) - 6 = 4(3x + 1)$ **[1]**

$\quad 15x + 5 - 6 = 12x + 4$

$\qquad\quad 3x - 1 = 4$ **[1]**

$\qquad\qquad 3x = 5$

$\qquad\qquad\; x = 1.667$ **[1]**

3. $4(2x - 1) = 3(3x - 2)$ **[1]**

$\quad 8x - 4 = 9x - 6$

$\quad 8x + 2 = 9x$ **[1]**

$\qquad 2 = x \text{ or } x = 2$ **[1]**

4. $(x + 10)(x - 1) = 0$ **[1]**

$x + 10 = 0 \text{ or } x - 1 = 0$ **[1]**

$x = -10$ **[1]** $\text{ or } x = 1$ **[1]**

Pages 176–177

Symmetry and Enlargement

1. a)   **b)**   **c)**   **[3]**

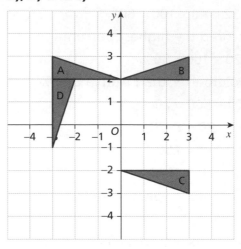

2. a), b) and **c)**

    [3]

d) 180° about the point (0, 0)   **[1]**

3. a) Shapes A and D are congruent.   **[1]**

    b) Shapes B and C are similar.   **[1]**

1.

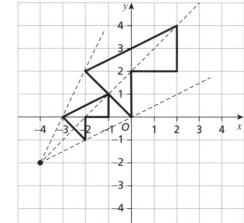

[1 mark for correct size of enlargement; 1 mark for correct position]

2. Scale factor is 2.5

Wing span = 20 ÷ 2.5 **[1]** = 8cm **[1]**

3. Translation by vector $\begin{pmatrix} 3 \\ 1 \end{pmatrix}$ **[1]**, then rotation **[1]** 90° anticlockwise **[1]** from the point (0, 3) **[1]**

Pages 178–179

Ratio and Proportion

1. a) 5 : 8 **[1]**
    b) 6 : 7 **[1]**
    c) 2 : 3 **[1]**
    d) 1 : 5 **[1]**
2. 700 ÷ 7 = 100 **[1]**
    3 parts = 100 × 3 = 300g
    4 parts = 100 × 4 = 400g
    = 300g : 400g **[1]**
3. £16 ÷ 2 = £8
    The larger share = £8 × 5 = £40 **[1]**
    Total amount to be shared
    = £16 + £40 = £56 **[1]**
4. 12 cupcakes × 2.5 = 30 cupcakes

    > Multiply each ingredient by 2.5

    Butter: 2.5 × 100g = 250g
    Sugar: 2.5 × 100g = 250g
    Flour: 2.5 × 100g = 250g **[1]**
    Baking powder: $2.5 \times \frac{1}{2}$ tsp = 1.25tsp
    Vanilla: $2.5 \times \frac{1}{2}$ tsp = 1.25tsp **[1]**
    Milk: 2.5 × 20ml = 50ml **[1]**
    Eggs: 2.5 × 2 = 5 eggs **[1]**
5. 3000 ÷ 5 = 600 **[1]**
    12 × 600 = 7200 **[1]**
6. a) £25.20 ÷ 6 = £4.20 **[1]**
    £4.20 × 8 = £33.60 **[1]**
    b) £63 ÷ £4.20 **[1]** = 15 hours **[1]**

1. a) £140 ÷ 7 = £20 **[1]**
    Ann saves 2 parts = 2 × £20 = £40 **[1]**
    b) 1 part = £52 ÷ 2 = £26 **[1]**
    Ann earns 7 parts = £26 × 7 = £182 **[1]**
2. 1 pencil costs £2 ÷ 8 = 25p **[1]**
    3 pencils cost 25p × 3 = 75p **[1]**
3.

Direct proportion		Inverse proportion	
A	D	B	C

[2]

4. x + 2x + x + 3 = 42 **[1]**
    4x + 3 = 42
    4x = 39
    x = 9.75 **[1]**
    Sand is 2x so 9.75 × 2 = 19.5kg **[1]**

Pages 180–181

Real-Life Graphs and Rates

1. a) 32km (± 1km) **[1]**
    b) John drives 40 miles = 64km, Alan drives
    60km **[1]**
    John drives 4km further **[1]**
    or John drives 40 miles, Alan drives
    60km = 37.5 miles **[1]**
    John drives 2.5 miles further. **[1]**
2. a) 50km **[1]**
    b) 30 minutes *or* $\frac{1}{2}$ hr **[1]**
    c) Speed = total distance ÷ total time
    s = 100km ÷ 2.5h **[1]** = 40km/h **[1]**

1. 15 minutes = 0.25h
    d = 30 × 2.25 **[1]** = 67.5 miles **[1]**
2. 12 minutes = 0.2h
    s = 5 ÷ 0.2 **[1]** = 25mph **[1]**
3.

    > Change 240km to miles.

    5 miles = 8km
    150 miles = 240km **[1]**
    Alia takes 3h 20mins to get to the
    airport = $3\frac{1}{3}$ h **[1]**
    Speed = $150 \div 3\frac{1}{3}$ **[1]**
    = 45 miles per hour **[1]**
4. a) UK: £75 = 1.25 × 75 **[1]** = €93.75 –
    cheaper in Spain **[1]**
    or Spain: €80 = 80 ÷ 1.25 **[1]**
    = £64 – cheaper in Spain **[1]**
    b) €13.75 *or* £11 cheaper **[1]**
5.

    > Change the units to metres first.

    Volume of gold bar = $l \times w \times h$ =
    0.25 × 0.8 × 0.2 = 0.04m³ **[1]**
    Density = mass ÷ volume =
    350 ÷ 0.04 **[1]** = 8750kg/m³ **[1]**

6.

Write down the equivalent change first.

£1.80 = €2.20 [1]

The exchange rate is (÷1.80) £1 = €1.22 [1]

Pages 182–183

Right-Angled Triangles

1. **a)** $12^2 + 17^2 = p^2$

$144 + 289 = 433$ [1]

$p = \sqrt{433} = 20.8$cm [1]

b) $1.3^2 + q^2 = 8.4^2$

$q^2 = 70.56 - 1.69$ [1]

$q = \sqrt{68.87} = 8.3$cm [1]

2. **A**

$16^2 + 12^2 = 20^2$

$256 + 144 = 400$

Yes, Pythagoras works. [1]

B

$18^2 + 11^2 = 21^2$

$324 + 121 = 445$, NOT 441

No [1]

C

$1.6^2 + 6.3^2 = 6.5^2$

$2.56 + 39.69 = 42.25$

Yes, Pythagoras works. [1]

3. $7^2 + 24^2 = c^2$

$49 + 576 = 625$

$c = \sqrt{625} = 25$cm [1]

Now use the second triangle:

$y^2 + 20^2 = 25^2$ [1]

$y^2 = 625 - 400$

$y = \sqrt{225} = 15$cm [1]

4. **a)** 0.87 [1]

b) 16.58 [1]

c) 21.42 [1]

5. **a)** $\tan 67° = 15 \div x$

$x = 15 \div \tan 67°$

$x = 6.4$cm [1]

b) $\cos x° = 39 \div 57$

$x = \cos^{-1}(39 \div 57)$

$x = 46.8°$ [1]

1. **a)** $\sin 16° = BC \div 25$

$BC = \sin 16° \times 25$ [1]

$BC = 6.9$m [1]

b) **i)** $\sin 21° = 6.9 \div$ ramp

ramp $= 6.9 \div \sin 21°$ [1]

ramp $= 19.3$m [1]

ii)

Here you must use the height.

$\tan 21° = 6.9 \div AC$

$AC = 6.9 \div \tan 21°$ [1]

$AC = 18.0$m [1]

2. $(6x)^2 + h^2 = (10x)^2$ or $6x$ [1]

$h^2 = 100x^2 - 36x^2$ [1]

$h^2 = 64x^2$ [1]

$h = \sqrt{64x^2} = 8x$ [1]

Pages 184–200

Mixed Test-Style Questions

No Calculator Allowed

1. **a)** 28 [1]

b) The median is between 25 and 27,
so is 26. [1]

c) The mean [1] and range [1]

2.

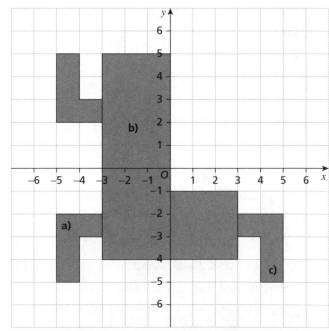

a) Reflection [1]

b) Enlargement [2]

c) Rotation [2]

3. a) **[2]** and b) **[2]**

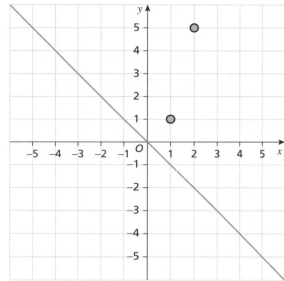

c) (3, 1) *or* (5, 2) *or* (0, 5) **[1]**

4. a) $\frac{8}{15}$ **[1]**

b) $1 - \frac{3}{15}$ **[1]** $= \frac{12}{15} = \frac{4}{5}$ **[1]**

c) $\frac{3}{14}$ **[1]**

5. Set 1: $\frac{1}{4} = 25\% = 0.25$ **[1]**

Set 2: $\frac{3}{5} = 60\% = 0.6$ **[1]**

Set 3: $\frac{11}{20} = 55\% = 0.55$ **[1]**

6. a) $a + 2b$ **[2] [1 mark for 2a+4b]**

b) 8 **[2] [1 mark for 32]**

7. In card B $p = 3$, NOT 4 **[1]**

8. a) £9.75 **[1]**

b) £10 **[1]**

c) 35% **[1]**

d) £20 **[1]**

9. $x = 3$ **[2] [1 mark for 25 and 100]**

10.

[1 mark for correct position on *x*-axis;
1 mark for correct position on *y*-axis]

11. Calcs R Us: 15% of £7 = 15 ÷ 100 × 7 = £1.05

Each calculator costs £7 − £1.05 = £5.95 **[1]**

12 calculators cost £5.95 × 12 = £71.40 **[1]**

ABC Calcs: 3 calculators cost 2 × £7.50 = £15

12 calculators cost £15 × 4 = £60 **[1]**

ABC Calcs are cheaper by £11.40 **[1]**

12. $4x + 12 = 40$ **[1]**

$4x = 28$ **[1]**

$x = 7$ **[1]**

13. $\frac{3}{8} + \frac{1}{5} = \frac{23}{40}$ **[1]**

$1 - \frac{23}{40} = \frac{17}{40}$ **[1]**

14. a) $x + 40 + 3x - 10 + 2x = 180°$ **[1]**

$6x + 30 = 180°$

$6x = 150°$

$x = 25°$ **[1]**

Largest angle 65° **[1]**

b) Isosceles triangle **[1]**

15.

Expression	Could it be the nth term?	5th term
$3n + 1$	✗	
$2(n^2 + 1)$	✓	52
$n + 6$	✗	
$2n^2 + 2$	✓	52

[1 mark for each correct row]

16. a) 4 multiplied by any number less than 1 including 0 as example **[1]**

b) Only 0 as example **[1]**

c) No, plus any correct counter example, e.g. $1^3 = 1$ **[1]**

17.

[1]

18. a) 30 [1]

   b) 8.5 [1]

   c) 17.5 [1]

19. a) $8^2 = 64$ and $9^2 = 81$, so $\sqrt{75}$ is between

      8 and 9 [1]

   b) 20 and 21 [2]

20. a) $\frac{6}{77}$ [1]

   b) $\frac{3}{45} = \frac{1}{15}$ [1]

   c) $\frac{32}{7}$ or $4\frac{4}{7}$ [1]

21. a) $180 - 40 = 140$

      $140 \div 2 = 70$ [1]

      $180 - 70 = 110°$ [1]

   b) $180 - 90 = 90$ [1]

      $90 - 63 = 27°$ [1]

22. a)

[1]

   b) Order 2 [1]

Mixed Test-Style Questions

Calculator Allowed

1. a) $350 \times 12 \times 250$ **[1]** $= 1\,050\,000\,\text{mm}^3$ **[1]**

   b) $\pi \times 14^2 \times 46$ **[1]** $= 28\,324.6\,\text{cm}^3$ **[1]**

   c) $\pi \times 1.6^2 \times 0.4$ **[1]** $= 3.22\,\text{m}^3$ **[1]**

2. a)

> Opposite angles in a parallelogram
> are equal.

      $360 - 105 - 105 = 150°$ [1]

      $150 \div 2 = 75°$ [1]

   b) $180 - 10 = 170$, $170 \div 2 = 85°$ [1]

      $180 - 85 = 95°$ [1]

3. C plus 5220 is greater than 5160 and 4200
[3] *or* C plus 435 is greater than 430 and
350. **[3]**

**[2 marks for any two of 5220, 5160, 4200,
435, 430 and 350; 1 mark for any one of
5220, 5160, 4200, 435, 430 and 350]**

4. $650 \div 5 \times 3$ **[1]** $= 390\,\text{cm}$ **[1]**

5. a) $40 \times £3.60 = £144$

      $£3.60 \times 0.4 = £1.44$ [1]

      Overtime rate $= £3.60 + £1.44 = £5.04$ [1]

      Overtime $= 5 \times £5.04 = £25.20$

      Amount earned in the week

      $= £144 + £25.20 = £169.20$ [1]

   b) $£169.20 \times 0.3 = £50.76$ [1]

      Take home pay $= £169.20 - £50.76 =$

      $£118.44$ [1]

6. Crowns: 0.2 [1]

   Jesters: 0.15

   Castles: 0.15 [1]

   Kings: 0.25

   Queens: 0.25 [1]

7. **A:** $3^2 + 4^2 = 5^2$

   $9 + 16 = 25$

   Yes [1]

   B: $8^2 + 15^2 = 17^2$

   $64 + 225 = 289$

   Yes [1]

   C: $17^2 + 16^2 = 23^2$

   $289 + 256 \ne 529$

   No [1]

   D: $60^2 + 11^2 = 61^2$

   $3600 + 121 = 3721$

   Yes [1]

8. a) $6x = 48$, $x = 8$ [1]

   b) $4x = -12$, $x = -3$ [1]

9. a) 10 litres of yellow [1]

   b) 20 litres of yellow [1]

   c) 12.5 litres of yellow [1]

10. $4.2 \times 0.8 \times 0.5 = 1.68$ [1]

   $0.3 \times 3.5 \times 0.5 = 0.525$ [1]

   $1.68 - 0.525 = 1.155\,\text{m}^3$ [1]

11. $500 \times 1.32 = €660$ [1]

12. a) $\frac{1}{4}(x + 12)$ [1]

   b) $2(x + 12)$ [1]

   c) $\frac{1}{8}$ [1]

13. a) Shortbread (35% compared to cookies

      31%) [1]

   b) $35 - 31 = 4\%$ more [1]

   [Allow ±1% in answer]

14. a) $\tan 40° = h \div 6$ **[1]**

> Remember that the vertical height will bisect the base.

$\tan 40° \times 6 = h = 5.03\text{cm}$ **[1]**

b) $\cos 40° = 6 \div \text{hypotenuse}$ **[1]**

$\text{hypotenuse} = 6 \div \cos 40° = 7.83\text{cm}$ **[1]**

15. a)

x	−3	−2	−1	0	1
y	−15	−11	−7	−3	1

[2 marks if all correct; 1 mark for three correct]

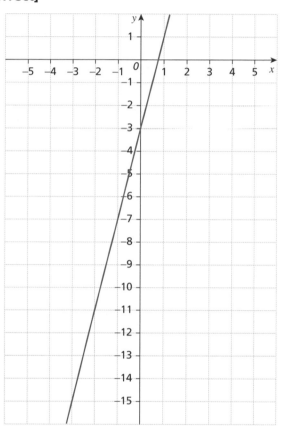

[2 marks for correct intercept and line]

b) 13 **[1]**

c) 7 **[1]**

16. $3x + 3 = 2 + 8 - 4x$ **[1]**

$7x + 3 = 10$ **[1]**

$7x = 7$

$x = 1$ **[1]**

17. a) $6 \div 18 \times 12$ **[1]**

> Remember: divide to find one, then times for all.

$= 4 \text{ cups of sugar}$ **[1]**

b) $8 \div 18 \times 12$ **[1]**

$= 5.333 = 5 \text{ cups of dried fruit}$ **[1]**

c) 6 cups of butter make 18 cakes

1 cup of butter makes 3 cakes **[1]**

9 cups of butter make $3 \times 9 = 27$ cakes **[1]**

18. a) i) \$3 **[1]**

ii) \$16 **[1]**

iii) \$320 **[1]**

b) i) £5 **[1]**

ii) £25 **[1]**

19. $\sin 35° = h \div 22$ **[1]**

$\sin 35° \times 22 = h = 12.6\text{m}$ **[1]**

20.

[3]

21. a) $\text{Density} = \text{mass} \div \text{volume} = 350 \div 0.04$ **[1]** $= 8750\text{kg/m}^3$ **[1]**

b) $\text{Density} = 900 \div 0.2$ **[1]** $= 4500\text{kg/m}^3$ **[1]**

22. a)

Item	Frequency	Estimated probability
Clothing	78	$\frac{78}{200} = 0.39$
Games	24	$\frac{24}{200} = 0.12$
Bric-a-brac	32	$\frac{32}{200} = 0.16$
Books	41	$\frac{41}{200} = 0.205$
Other	25	$\frac{25}{200} = 0.125$

[2 marks for all correct; 1 mark for at least three correct]

b) $0.39 + 0.12 = 0.51$ **[1]**

$0.205 + 0.16 = 0.365$, so books and bric-a-brac less likely **[1]**

c) $500 \times 0.205 = 102.5$ books **[1]**

Accept 103 or 102 as whole books **[1]**

23. Yes. [1]
    Two pairs of sides and the angle between
    them are equal (SAS). [1]
    or:
    Two pairs of angles and the side between
    them are equal (ASA). [1]